# A
# CONSTITUTIONAL
# CONVENTION

## Threat or Challenge?

## Wilbur Edel

PRAEGER SPECIAL STUDIES • PRAEGER SCIENTIFIC

Library of Congress Cataloging in Publication Data

Edel, Wilbur.
     A constitutional convention.

     (Praeger scientific)
     Bibliography: p.
     Includes index.
     1. Constitutional conventions--United States.
I. Title.
KF4555.E33        342.73'032        80-27573
ISBN 0-03-059073-6

Published in 1981 by Praeger Publishers
CBS Educational and Professional Publishing
A Division of CBS, Inc.
521 Fifth Avenue, New York, New York 10175 U.S.A.

© 1981 by Praeger Publishers

123456789   145   987654321

Printed in the United States of America

# ACKNOWLEDGMENTS

I am grateful to the Ellen Clarke Bertrand Library of Bucknell University for making the library's excellent facilities and collections available to me. My special thanks go to assistant librarian Joel Clemmer, head of the reference section, and to the other members of the reference staff for the generous and ever-ready assistance they gave me in my search for documentary material. I appreciate the consideration given to my inquiries by members and former members of the United States Senate and House of Representatives. These legislators are identified in a special section of the bibliography listing personal correspondence from members of the Congress.

Permission to quote from the following modern studies and commentaries is gratefully acknowledged:

American Bar Association, Special Constitutional Convention Study Committee, "Amendment of the Constitution by the Convention Method under Article V" (1973). A quoted summary of the complaint filed in a suit to prevent ratification of the Equal Rights Amendment is reprinted from Student Lawyer, © 1980, American Bar Association.

American Enterprise Institute for Public Policy Research, "A Constitutional Convention: How Well Would It Work?" Transcript of a forum held 23 May 1979, Washington, D.C.

Charles L. Black, Jr., "The Proposed Amendment of Article V: A Threatened Disaster," quoted by permission of the Yale Law Journal Company and Fred B. Rothman & Company from the Yale Law Journal, vol. 72 (1963), p. 964.

Charles L. Black, Jr., "Amending the Constitution: A Letter to a Congressman," quoted by permission of the Yale Law Journal Company and Fred B. Rothman & Company from the Yale Law Journal, vol. 82 (1972), pp. 189, 195, 209.

Common Cause, "Constitutional Convention Is 'Great Unknown'," In Common, Winter 1979.

"Proposed Legislation on the Convention Method of Amending the United States Constitution" (Note), Harvard Law Review, vol. 85 (1972).

"Save Me a Seat at that Convention," Seattle Post-Intelligencer, 25 February 1979.

# CONTENTS

# INTRODUCTION

The clamor for amendments to the Constitution of the United States has given new impetus to a demand raised on a number of occasions since the American Revolution: that proposed changes in the country's basic law be considered by a national convention. This device, although used to design the present Constitution, and authorized under Article V of that Constitution as one method of initiating amendments, has never been utilized since its adoption in 1787.

In the two decades from 1960 to 1980, proponents of new amendments, most notably those that would mandate a balanced federal budget, insure equal rights for women (ERA), and prohibit federal support of abortions or of school busing, have pressed their demands upon Congress with increasing fervor. Only ERA has followed the traditional amendment procedure of a congressional resolution subsequently submitted to state legislatures for ratification. Supporters of each of the other proposals have insisted that, if Congress does not take the initiative, a constitutional convention must be called to approve the desired amendment. The proposal to revive the convention system is a frightening one to many who are fearful of the potential dangers in using an amendment procedure about which so many questions have been raised but not answered.

This study reviews the country's experience with constitutional amendment procedures, and considers the implications of that experience in terms of the problems that will arise when Congress is forced to a decision by the demands of two-thirds of the state legislatures for a constitutional convention. It also examines the arguments for and against legislation to establish convention regulations, and offers an evaluation of this and other approaches to the convention problem.

Because the historical significance of much of the evidence considered here is best illustrated by the exact words of the participants in this aspect of the United States' development, extensive use has been made of direct quotations. For example, to insure not only accuracy but also completeness in reviewing the framers' intent with respect to the powers of a constitutional convention, I have included all of James Madison's notes relating to debates on the amendment process in the Philadelphia convention of 1787. Similarly, key points made by later observers, whether officeholders or students of politics, frequently are reported in the words of the individual rather than in paraphrased versions that might distort the original meaning. For reference purposes, most direct quotations are cited separately in the notes, though occasionally a single citation may be used for a series of quotations taken from successive pages in one source document.

# A NOTE ABOUT SOURCE MATERIALS

Books, articles, and documentary collections are cited in the notes by author and title only, with dates added where appropriate. A complete citation for each source used is included in the bibliography. Congressional resolutions and bills are identified by number and are referenced by volume and page in the Congressional Record. Abbreviated citation references for sources used repeatedly in this volume are as follows:

ABA—American Bar Association, Special Constitutional Convention Study Committee, "Amendment of the Constitution by the Convention Method under Article V" (1973).

Ames—Herman Ames, The Proposed Amendments to the Constitution of the United States during the First Century of its History (1970 reprint of study first published in 1896).

BB Hearing—U.S. Senate, Committee on the Judiciary, Subcommittee on Constitutional Amendments, Hearing on Balancing the Budget (94th Cong., 1st sess., 1975).

CR—Congressional Record

CR (daily)—References found in the daily issues of the Congressional Record, rather than the bound volumes, principally for the years 1976 through 1980.

Docs—Library of Congress, Documents Illustrative of the Formation of the Union of American States (1927).

ERA Hearings—U.S. House of Representatives, Committee on the Judiciary, Subcommittee on Civil and Constitutional Rights, Hearings on Equal Rights Amendment Extension (95th Cong., 1st and 2d sess., 1977-78).

Farrand—Max Farrand, ed., The Records of the Federal Convention of 1787 (1923).

FCC Hearings—U.S. Senate, Committee on the Judiciary, Subcommittee on Separation of Powers, Hearings on a Federal Constitutional Convention (90th Cong., 1st sess., 1967).

Poore—Ben Perley Poore, The Federal and State Constitutions, Colonial Charters, and Other Organic Laws of the United States, 2d ed. (1878).

# ARTICLE V

The Congress, whenever two-thirds of both Houses shall deem it necessary, shall propose amendments to this Constitution, or, on the application of the legislatures of two-thirds of the several States, shall call a convention for proposing amendments, which, in either case, shall be valid to all intents and purposes, as part of this Constitution when ratified by the legislatures of three-fourths of the several States, or by conventions in three-fourths thereof, as the one or the other mode of ratification may be proposed by the Congress; Provided that [no amendment which may be made prior to the year one thousand eight hundred and eight shall in any manner affect the first and fourth·clauses in the ninth section of the first article; and that] no State, without its consent, shall be deprived of its equal suffrage in the Senate.

---

*The italicized section is the only procedure never used since the Constitution was adopted. The bracketed portion is no longer effective, having been negated by time and amendments to other parts of the Constitution.

# 1
## WHY A CONSTITUTIONAL CONVENTION?

Over the first two centuries of American independence, thousands of proposals have been made to modify the Constitution that was designed by members of a national convention held in Philadelphia in 1787.[1] Except for that complete rewriting of the nation's basic law, all changes but one have been made by what has become the traditional method of amendment: initiation by a two-thirds majority of both houses of Congress, followed by ratification by the legislatures of three-fourths of the states. This tradition was broken only once when, in 1933, Congress directed that a proposal to repeal the Eighteenth Amendment (Prohibition) be submitted to state conventions for ratification rather than to state legislatures.[2] The only process that never has been used is the one that permits a national convention to initiate amendments. Authority for this procedure is found in the italicized portion of Article V printed above.

## CONVENTIONS IN COLONIAL AND POSTREVOLUTIONARY TIMES

The country's lack of experience in the use of a national convention to propose constitutional amendments has not been the result of disinterest in this method. Long before independence had been achieved—or even sought—settlers in several of the colonies had resorted to conventions to establish the basic principles and forms of self-government. Although local autonomy often was inhibited by the terms of royal charters and proprietary grants, there were numerous occasions in which weak controls or changes in the British monarchy gave the colonists opportunities to organize according to

1

their own preferences. Such an opportunity occurred during the early years of settlement in Connecticut. Émigrés from Massachusetts Bay, seeking greater freedom than the narrow religious leadership of Massachusetts permitted, relocated in an area north of Long Island Sound. Beginning with locally elected leaders in each community, residents of the towns of Hartford, Wethersfield, and Windsor assembled in 1639 for the express purpose of adopting a common system of government. The Hartford convention, as it came to be known, produced the "Fundamental Orders of Connecticut," frequently referred to as the first written constitution to establish a popular government.[3] More than this, it was the first governing instrument in America that acknowledged no higher earthly authority than the voters of the federated towns. The objective of these colonists was declared to be "an orderly and decent government established according to God," not the King of England.

No action was taken by the British government to intervene in the matter of Connecticut's political organization until 1662, when Charles II issued a charter to the "Governor and Company of the English Colony of Connecticut."[4] Like the earlier Charter of New England that had been granted the Plymouth Company, the provisions for electing local representatives were such that when the colonies revolted more than a century later, both Connecticut and Massachusetts were able to continue functioning under their royal charters, by legislation substituting the name of the state for the name of the British monarch, until new constitutions could be written.[5]

The same decade that produced the Fundamental Orders of Connecticut saw suggestions for a New England federation. Although limited to Connecticut and Massachusetts "plantations," this early proposal for "Articles of Confederation" was drafted by representatives from both areas, and established a pattern for cooperative action that would culminate in the thirteen-colony congress that produced the Declaration of Independence.

A revolutionary and postrevolutionary history has demonstrated, the convention tradition owes as much to the states as to activity at the federal level. Even as the Continental Congress was working out the details of the country's first constitution—the Articles of Confederation—individual colonies were engaged in writing state constitutions. This was encouraged by Congress which, prior to its adoption of a formal declaration of independence, approved on May 15, 1776 what John Adams characterized as "the most important resolution that ever was taken in America." Opening with a preamble stating that the government of Great Britain had excluded the colonies from its protection and was threatening them with destruction by force of arms, Congress reached the following conclusion:

That it be recommended to the respective Assemblies and
Conventions of the United Colonies, where no government
sufficient to the exigencies of their affairs has been hither-
to established, to adopt such government as shall in the
opinion of the representatives of the people best conduce
to the happiness and safety of their constituents in particular, and America in general.

Commenting on the resolution in a personal letter, Caesar Rodney of
Delaware observed: "Most of those here who are termed the <u>cool</u>
<u>considerate men</u> think it amounts to a declaration of independence"
[Rodney's emphasis]. [6]

Even in colonies whose leaders objected to the preamble because
its denunciation of Great Britain seemed to close the door to reconcil-
iation, there was support for the proposal to set up new governments.
Several began this task almost at once, Virginia concluding preparation of its fundamental law June 29, and New Jersey approving a
government and constitution July 2. In the months following official
proclamation of the Declaration of Independence, elected conventions
met in Delaware, Georgia, Maryland, New Hampshire, North Carolina, and Pennsylvania, each establishing a government within the
framework of a formal constitution. [7] By November 15, 1777, when
Congress completed work on the Articles of Confederation, only
Massachusetts and Rhode Island had not adopted constitutions. Only
in Connecticut, South Carolina, and Virginia were constitutions prepared by the established legislatures. [8]

Thanks to the requirement of unanimity, ratification of the
Articles of Confederation required another three and one-half years.
By March 1, 1781, when this compact became effective, the convention system was well established in most states. Of the three exceptions, Connecticut's first constitution was "enacted and declared by
the Governor, and Council, and House of Representatives, in General
Court Assembled. "[9] But when the neighboring Massachusetts legislature attempted to adopt a constitution of its own making in 1778,
the plan was rejected by the voters. The following year a convention
was called and the document prepared by that body was approved by
more than two-thirds of the electorate. [10]

On the national scene, the federal government organized under
the Articles of Confederation found itself severely handicapped in
many areas, not the least of which was management of the country's
commerce. Not only was the government (that is, the Congress)
unable to convince other nations of the desirability of concluding
commercial treaties with the United States, it was further embar-
rassed by its inability to control commercial relations among the

states. When an effort to deal specifically with the matter of interstate commerce failed, the suggestion for a broader attack on the
constitutional problem was coupled with a recommendation that a
special convocation of state representatives be called for this purpose.[11] Congress might issue the invitations, but a separately
selected convention would consider the problem—albeit a convention
of delegates chosen by the several state legislatures—and would make
its proposals for constitutional change. Congress accepted this recommendation with remarkable promptness on February 21, 1787, only
five months after having received and turned over to a congressional
committee the report of the Annapolis convention.[12]

When the constitutional convention met at Philadelphia in 1787,
it gave scant attention to the question of the procedure to be used in
future modifications of the new constitution. Moreover, until a week
before the convention finished its work, it appeared that the convention method for framing amendments would be the only one permitted.
This approach stemmed from a plan submitted during the first days
of the convention by Edmund Randolph of Virginia. The Virginia Plan
contained a very brief section suggesting only that "provision ought
to be made for the amendment of the Articles of Union whensoever it
shall seem necessary." It contained no instructions as to procedure,
except to advise that "the assent of the national legislature ought not
to be required."[13] Although the phrase that would have excluded
Congress from the amendment process was deleted early in convention deliberations,[14] when the first specific procedure was proposed
by a Committee of Detail, it provided only for amendment by a convention that was to be called by Congress on the request of two-thirds
of the state legislatures.[15] This was approved without opposition.[16]
Not until the last week of the convention was the article revised to
include an alternative to the convention method.[17]

Even delegates most fearful of action by "the people"—like
Elbridge Gerry of Massachusetts and Alexander Hamilton of New
York—did not oppose initiation of amendments by convention until
James Madison of Virginia suggested the difficulties this would create.
Madison's substitute article, which gave initial responsibility to
Congress and contained no reference to a convention, was at first
approved by a vote of nine states to one.[18] When the Committee of
Style presented an updated document with this revised version a few
days later, Madison's Virginia colleague, George Mason, expressed
outrage at the change that he said would take the matter out of the
hands of the people and leave it entirely under the control of Congress.
Mason denounced the revision as reflecting "a doctrine utterly subversive of the fundamental principles of the rights and liberties of
the people.[19] Only then was agreement reached on restoration of the

convention as one method—but no longer the sole method—for initiating amendments.[20]

Apart from Article V, in which the amendment process acknowledges indirectly the voters' right to participate (indirectly) in decisions on constitutional change, only the preamble of the U.S. Constitution refers to "the people" as a party to the design of the nation's fundamental law. When compared to the more specific language in many state constitutions, the federal document produced by the Philadelphia convention contains a relatively restrained statement, announcing in its preamble:

> We, the people of the United States, in order to form a
> more perfect union, establish justice, insure domestic
> tranquility, provide for the common defence, promote
> the general welfare, and secure the blessings of liberty
> to ourselves and our posterity, do ordain and establish
> this constitution for the United States of America.

Both before and after the adoption of the federal constitution, state constitutions were designed to include more particular statements of the principle that the people are the ultimate source of all political authority. As an example, the longest paragraph in the brief Connecticut constitution of 1776 was this introductory declaration:

> The people of this state, being by the providence of God,
> free and independent, have the sole and exclusive right
> of governing themselves as a free, sovereign, and inde-
> pendent state; and having from their ancestors derived a
> free and excellent constitution of government whereby
> the legislature depends on the free and annual election
> of the people, they have the best security for the preser-
> vation of their civil and religious rights and liberties.[21]

Maryland's 1776 constitution made the point more succinctly in the first article of a "declaration of rights" rather than in a preamble, stating that "all government of right originates from the people, is founded in compact only, and instituted solely for the good of the whole."[22]

Other states went one step further, borrowing from the Declaration of Independence the right-of-revolution doctrine that was carefully avoided by the members of the Philadelphia convention. Some did this by means of lengthy descriptions of the need for a new constitution, reciting the colony's grievances against Great Britain in much the same fashion as Congress had done in the Declaration of Independence.[23] A few used the declaration of rights as a vehicle for defining the principle of popular sovereignty as the right to abolish and completely reconstruct an unsatisfactory government or political system. Perhaps the earliest and most forcefully stated example of this view is found in "A declaration of the rights made by the representatives of the good people of Virginia, assembled in full and free convention." Although the "convention" in this case consisted of 45 members of the colonial House of Burgesses who had not been elected to prepare a constitution, that body nevertheless produced in June 1776 both a constitution and, as a separate document, a declaration of rights that contained the following paragraphs:

> Sec. 2. That all power is vested in, and consequently derived from, the people. . . .
> Sec. 3. That government is, or ought to be, instituted for the common benefit, protection, and security of the people, nation, or community . . . when any government shall be found inadequate or contrary to these purposes, a majority of the community hath an indubitable, inalienable, and indefeasible right to reform, alter or abolish it, in such manner as shall be judged most conducive to the public weal[24] (emphasis added).

This revolutionary doctrine did not appear as frequently in constitutions written after independence had been won and a treaty recognizing that fact had been signed by Great Britain. But it persisted for a time, reappearing in Connecticut's first postrevolutionary constitution and in the constitutions of some of the new states that entered the Union during the first half of the nineteenth century. Alabama in 1819, Arkansas in 1836, and California in 1849 applied for statehood with constitutions that repeated in essentially the same form the "inalienable right" of the people to alter or abolish any government that did not serve the purposes for which it had been established.[25]

Notwithstanding these ringing declarations of democratic principle, most states adopted a more conservative approach to the operation and control of government, including the process of constitutional amendment. Eight of the thirteen original constitutions— including that designed by the Virginia legislature—contained no provision for amendment. Of the five that did acknowledge the need for such a procedure, two (those of Delaware and Maryland) designated the legislature as the body having exclusive jurisdiction in this area.[26] (Although the notion of popular participation in the process of constitutional change, either indirectly through specially elected conventions or directly in ratifying referenda, appeared frequently as one element of the amendment procedure, just as frequently—often in the same constitution—the legislature was designated as the agency responsible for initiating amendments or proposing a convention.) Georgia directed its legislature to call a convention if petitions requesting one were received "from a majority of counties . . . signed by a majority of voters in each county . . . ."[27] Massachusetts, anticipating the need for a complete review before the turn of the century, provided that in 1795 the legislature was to have the towns canvass their voters "for the purpose of collecting their sentiments on the necessity or expediency of revising the constitution," and to call for an election of delegates to a convention if two-thirds of the voters favored a revision.[28] Pennsylvania, the fifth of the original states to design an amendment procedure, initially adopted a kind of monitoring system that provided for the election every seven years of a "Council of Censors." This council would have the power to review all operations of government and to call for the election of a convention "if there appear to them an absolute necessity of amending any article of the constitution which may be defective."[29]

## ATTITUDES TOWARD CONVENTIONS IN THE NINETEENTH CENTURY

Common acceptance of the general principle of popular sovereignty permitted changes in state constitutions even where no specific amendment process was provided. Virginia, for example, went through major revisions in 1830 and 1850 without feeling any necessity for incorporating in its constitution the process that in fact was used on both occasions: a convention called by the legislature, whose work subsequently was ratified by popular vote.[30] The convention of 1829-30 did, however, bring into focus the limitations of the revolutionary doctrine that Virginia had been foremost in establishing, and to which it continued giving lip service in its bill of rights.

Like most states of that time, Virginia maintained a severely restricted voting franchise. Attempts to extend the suffrage from property owners to taxpayers, and to give the less affluent residents of the western counties proportionate representation in the legislature, were beaten back by the eastern Tidewater establishment. Similarly, entrenched conservatives in all states fought to protect the traditionally limited system of suffrage. One of the most striking examples was the action of New York's 1821 convention in effectively disenfranchising 30,000 free negroes who previously had the same voting privileges as whites.[31]

In Virginia, the same landed gentry who prevented the 1829-30 convention from approving more than a token extension of suffrage, also defeated an effort to add an amendment article to the constitution.

The absence of such a provision was one of many aspects of the 1776 constitution that had long been under fire from Thomas Jefferson. But Jefferson had died three years before the 1829 convention was called, and even former supporters of his views joined in a concert of scornful derision of the recommendations attributed to him. On the particular subject of an amendment article, John Randolph (no relation to Edmund Randolph) castigated "this maggot of innovation" as making as much sense as a marriage contract with a provision for divorce.[32] In the face of this kind of opposition, the amendment provision was overwhelmingly defeated.[33]

In other states, constitutional revisions occurred much earlier and, in some cases, more frequently. Delaware, Georgia, New Hampshire, and South Carolina modified their revolutionary constitutions before 1800, Georgia and South Carolina each going through this process twice during the years from 1778 to 1798.[34] The act by which South Carolina first revised its constitution referred to the earlier document as one intended to be "temporary only." New states entering the union during the first three decades after the installation of the nation's federal government followed what had become the dominant pattern in two aspects of constitution-writing. With few exceptions, their constitutions were designed by popularly elected conventions and contained explicit provisions for amendment.[35] Congress not only acknowledged the popular basis of these petitions for statehood in its early enabling acts, it soon made the convention form of constitution-making a prerequisite for statehood. The acts of Congress that enabled Ohio, Louisiana, and other territories to organize as states, specified that a popularly elected convention draw up the proposed constitution and frame of government.[36] In some cases Congress went further and stipulated that the action of the convention be ratified by a subsequent vote of the people.[37] Both state use of constitutional conventions and congressional insistence on this procedure by new candidates for statehood continued through the nineteenth century. The Civil War did not interrupt this practice, though the conventions called to rewrite the constitutions of states that seceded from the Union, and those convened by Union-appointed provisional governors to revise them again after the war, functioned under constraints not experienced in normal times.

In imposing the above-mentioned conditions upon territories petitioning for statehood, Congress concurred in the judgment of people at the state level that elected conventions were the most appropriate bodies for designing constitutions. As most new-state constitutions included the convention as one option in the amending process, Congress presumably accepted that procedure as a suitable one for bringing about constitutional change. Yet, as this and later chapters demonstrate, Congress discouraged or evaded every attempt to use the convention method for initiating changes in the federal constitution. Regardless of whether such suggestions came from the states or from members of Congress, they received little support in the national legislature.

Convention proposals began with applications from New York and Virginia almost immediately after the federal government had been established.[38] In the years that followed, other states petitioned for conventions, some because of concern over federal-state relations, others out of a desire to face a particular issue. In the early 1830s the legislature of South Carolina sent Congress a resolution asking that "a convention of the states be called as early as practicable to consider and determine such questions of disputed powers as have arisen between the States of this Confederacy and the General Government."[39] As the language suggests, South Carolina looked for a gathering similar to the one convened in 1787, not one of delegates elected by popular vote. The Delaware legislature was quick to point out that the federal Constitution "does not recognize any such tribunal or political assemblage as a convention of States."[40] As the Civil War approached, states in both the North and South petitioned for a convention that would resolve the problems that threatened open conflict, but to no avail. While the war was in progress, and notwithstanding the Article V provision that a convention be called "on the application of the legislatures of two-thirds of the several states," resolutions for "a convention of the states for the purpose of bringing about the restoration of peace and the Union" were introduced into Congress by Representative Clement L. Vallandigham of Ohio and Senator Garrett Davis of Kentucky.[41]

In later years, the character of state appeals for a national convention focused more frequently on specific issues or segments of the Constitution. The significance of these movements, particularly in the twentieth century, will be considered in later chapters.

Running parallel with state efforts to utilize the convention system for modification of the federal constitution were proposals by members of Congress. Some, like the plan for the convention of 1787, were intended to provide opportunities for reviewing the nation's general condition and updating the Constitution accordingly. In 1824 Representative Ebenezer Herrick of Maine proposed that amendments be considered every tenth year but be prohibited in the intervals between decades.[42] Almost a century later, Representative Walter M. Chandler of New York suggested a periodic review of the Constitution every 30 years.[43]

More commonly, proposals that would authorize action by convention have aimed at changing particular provisions of the Constitution. Some of these involved attempts to ease the process of amendment as laid down in Article V. On a number of occasions congressional

resolutions have been offered to reduce the size of the majority of
states required to call a convention. One of the earliest of these,
submitted in 1864 by Senator John B. Henderson of Missouri during
consideration of a resolution to abolish slavery, provided that:

> whenever a majority of the members elected to each
> House, or a convention called on the application of the
> legislatures of a majority of the several states, should
> propose amendments, these in either case should be
> valid when ratified by the legislatures of or conventions
> in two-thirds of the several states, as Congress should
> direct.[44]

Nine years later, a resolution by Representative Charles H. Porter
of Virginia introduced the notion of popular participation, recommending that "Congress, whenever three-fifths of both Houses of
Congress deem it necessary, may propose amendments to the Constitution, or may call a convention for proposing amendments and
revising the Constitution." Calling a convention would be mandated
"on the application of the legislatures of any number of states, em-
bracing three-fifths of the enumerated population of the several
states." Regardless of the method of initiation, amendments would
be valid "when approved and ratified by a majority of the electors
in the several states voting thereon, and qualified to vote for Representatives in Congress." As Herman Ames pointed out in his survey
of federal constitutional amendments, these resolutions proposed
"a system analogous to that adopted by many of the states for amending their constitutions."[45]

The 1860s saw other methods proposed that were common to
early state constitutions. One was to "take the sense of the people"
on amendments recommended by Congress. Another was offered by
Senator Garret Davis of Kentucky as an amendment to the Fifteenth
Amendment (extending the suffrage to former slaves). Senator Davis
proposed that all amendments be submitted to the people of each
state, with ratification "by a majority of the people entitled to vote
in three-fourths of the several states."[46]

TWENTIETH-CENTURY AMENDMENT PROPOSALS

Proposals for direct public participation in the amendment
process were encouraged during the early twentieth century by the
clamor for broadening the suffrage through direct election of senators
and by extension of the voting franchise to women. Individual members of Congress sponsored many plans that called for a constitutional

convention to initiate such changes. Senator Robert L. Owen of Oklahoma, at regular intervals from 1911 to 1923, introduced a resolution to amend Article V to permit a simple majority of both houses of Congress to call a convention and to mandate a popular vote to ratify or reject the convention's work. Other aspects of the Owen plan were more complicated, but one feature recalls the early state constitutions' insistence on wide publication of proposed amendments with the names of legislators who have voted for or against them. Owen's proposal called for distributing to voters a pamphlet containing the arguments on both sides of a particular amendment, to be prepared by the leading congressional representatives of the two opposing views.[47] A 1914 suggestion from Representative William L. Igoe of Missouri would have permitted a convention to be called "on the petition of 10 per cent of the voters of a majority of the states," and stipulated that convention proposals be ratified by a national referendum in which "a majority of the votes in a majority of the states and a majority of the total votes in all states" would affirm the convention's decision.[48] More than twenty other plans embodying elements of direct public participation in the amendment process were submitted to Congress in later years, but none gained the approval of the national legislature.

One of the most radical revisions of Article V was proposed in 1913 by Representative Chandler. His resolution provided that a convention be called if at least one-fourth of the states, comprising one-fourth or more of the country's population, desired it, and that the legislatures of these states or "a majority of the electors voting thereon," be entitled to call a convention. Like Edmund Randolph, Chandler would have bypassed Congress completely in his procedure, which stipulated that ratification be by the majority of electors in the the majority of states.[49]

Equally radical, but in a very different sense, was a 1963 proposal of the Council of State Governments that would have permitted initiation of an amendment by the action of two-thirds of the state legislatures in approving "identical texts." Ironically, the council sought to use a national convention to eliminate both the convention system and Congress from the amendment process, and put both initiation and ratification in the hands of the state legislatures.[50]

The desire to circumvent Congress is one of the principal reasons for seeking action by a national convention. Throughout the life of the Republic, there has been a feeling that Congress might prove a stumbling block to constitutional change. The unrelenting efforts of Edmund Randolph and George Mason to establish the convention, rather than Congress, as the authority for proposing amendments, were based on their clearly stated view that Congress could not be relied on to fulfill this obligation, no matter how great the need. This distrust of the national legislature often went hand-in-hand with the notion that there should be greater popular participation in decisions to alter the country's basic law. Even without public action as direct as in a referendum, it was thought that delegates to a constitutional convention would reflect more accurately the electorate's views than members of a Congress who had been chosen for a great variety of reasons unrelated to the question of constitutional change. In his first inaugural address, Abraham Lincoln expressed a preference for the convention mode of amendment. He capsuled many of the reasons commonly offered in support of this method in his brief explanation that "it allows amendments to originate with the people themselves, instead of only permitting them to take or reject propositions originated by others, not especially chosen for the purpose, and which might not be precisely such as they would wish to either accept or reject."[51]

The two objectives of avoiding congressional opposition and making constitutional change subject to popular will have been largely responsible for the submission, since 1789, of approximately four hundred state petitions for a constitutional convention. More than half that number have been submitted since 1957, which suggests that impatience with congressional response to demands for amendments is increasing.[52] As one modern student of this subject has reported, a representative of the antibusing National Committee for a Constitutional Amendment declared in 1974: "So far, we have 18 states. If we get 34, we can amend the Constitution [by convention] and the heck with them in Washington."[53] This has been the attitude of an increasing number of organizations supporting single-issue campaigns for amendment of the Constitution.

Many members of Congress have introduced resolutions proposing amendments similar to those designed by private, special-interest groups, but few of these resolutions have been considered by the committees to which they have been referred as a normal first step in the legislative process. As a nineteenth-century researcher noted in a study published in 1896:

> Of the more than eighteen hundred propositions to amend the Constitution, introduced in Congress during the first century of its legislative history, over one-half have received no further consideration beyond their reception and reference to a committee. The remainder have either been reported or received further discussion, but only a very small percentage of these have been brought to a vote.[54]

In recent years the aversion of the Senate and House Judiciary Committees to any discussion of constitutional amendments or legislation affecting Article V has become even more pronounced. Without committee consideration, and subsequent approval, the possibility of a resolution being calendared for general debate by the full Senate or House of Representatives is remote. By comparison, pro-amendment groups have found state legislators much more receptive to their pleas, particularly when a proposed amendment would serve not only to limit the powers of Congress, but also to broaden the authority of state governments.

Causes that have shown strength on a countrywide basis have found many state legislatures willing to apply to Congress for a convention to effect the desired constitutional change. In this respect the mood has shifted from that of an earlier period, when public pressure convinced 26 state legislatures of the need for giving up their long-held power to select U.S. senators by asking for a convention to approve the election of senators by popular vote. On that occasion, Congress evaded the convention issue by initiating its own resolution which, after ratification by three-fourths of the states, became the seventeenth amendment.[55] The more recent appeals for a constitutional convention, ranging in purpose from moral issues such as abortion and school busing to pocketbook problems of taxation and budgeting, have put pressure on state and national legislators alike.[56] But it is at the state level that the convention campaigns have been most successful.

Since 1970, no problem has commanded more attention than deficit spending by the federal government. Unlike most campaigns for modification of the Constitution, the drive for a balanced-budget amendment has been accompanied by a demand from many states that the matter be put before a national convention. The degree of success achieved by supporters of this effort indicates that it will have a better chance of reaching its objective than any previous attempt. For this reason, it offers a good case for analysis of the problems involved in the calling and functioning of a constitutional convention.

Before considering this problem in a twentieth-century setting, one must examine the oft-repeated claim that the precedent for a constitutional convention was established in 1787 when Congress called for a national convention to revise the then-existing constitution, the Articles of Confederation. Although the tax revolt of the 1970s bears little resemblance to the movement that gave rise to the Philadelphia convention of 1787, it is important to look at that earlier experience to determine its applicability to modern conditions.

NOTES

1. A study by James Stasny, printed in CR (daily), 2 November 1977, pp. S18494-99, reports that published and unpublished records in the Senate library indicate that 9,210 amendments were proposed through August 1977.

2. The most complete study of the procedures used in ratifying the Twenty-first Amendment is Everett Sommerville Brown's Ratifi- fication of the Twenty-First Amendment to the Constitution of the United States.

3. Breckinridge Long, Genesis of the Constitution of the United States of America, pp. 29-34. For the text of the Fundamental Orders of Connecticut see Henry Steele Commager, ed. , Documents of Amer- ican History (2d ed. , 1940), pp. 23-24.

4. Poore, vol. 1, p. 252.

5. The first constitution adopted by Connecticut in 1776 was a five-paragraph statement that merely established the state's inde- pendence and set forth the basic freedoms guaranteed all individuals (ibid. , pp. 257-58). A more detailed document, similar to constitu- tions written by neighboring states, was framed in 1818 (ibid. , pp. 258-66). Massachusetts did not adopt a new constitution until 1780 (ibid. , pp. 956-73).

6. A facsimile of the resolution of 15 May 1776 appears in Library of Congress, Paul H. Smith, ed. , Letters of Delegates to Congress, vol. 3, p. 677. The comments of John Adams and Caesar Rodney are in vol. 3, p. 676 and vol. 4, p. 30, respectively. Reac- tions of other members of Congress are reflected in letters written during the first weeks after May 15 and reproduced in vol. 4, pp. 3- 70. Congress President John Hancock's letters conveying the recom- mendation of Congress to the Connecticut, New Hampshire, and Massachusetts legislatures are printed in vol. 4, pp. 6-7.

7. The first constitutions of New Jersey and Virginia appear in Poore, vol. 2, pp. 1310 and 1908; those of Delaware, Georgia, Maryland, New Hampshire, North Carolina, and Pennsylvania are in vol. 1, pp. 273, 377, 817, and vol. 2, pp. 1279, 1409, 1540.

8. Ibid. , vol. 1, p. 257 and vol. 2, pp. 1615, 1908.

9. Ibid. , vol. 1, p. 257. The term "General Court" was used in a number of states to refer collectively to the two houses of the legislature.

10. Ibid. , vol. 1, p. 956n.

11. "Proceedings of Commissioners to Remedy Defects of the Federal Government, " held at Annapolis, Maryland, 11-14 September 1786. Docs, pp. 39-43.

12. Ibid. , pp. 44-46, from Journals of the Continental Congress, vol. 38.

13. Docs, p. 119.

14. Ibid., p. 191.

15. Ibid., p. 481.

16. Ibid., p. 646.

17. The convention opened 25 May 1787 and first received the Virginia Plan from Randolph May 29. The section on amendment procedure was considered briefly on June 5, June 11, and July 23. No specific procedure was offered for discussion until August 30. September 10 saw the beginning of serious consideration of this point. A renewal of that discussion of September 15, the day the convention approved the entire Constitution, led to acceptance of Article V in its present form. A more detailed account of the evolution of Article V is provided in Chapter 2, which includes all of Madison's notes on the sessions devoted to the amendment process.

18. Docs, p. 697.

19. Farrand, vol. 2, p. 629, n.8.

20. Docs, p. 735. Several years later Thomas Jefferson wrote the following account of this development as related to him by George Mason (original punctuation modified for clarity): "The cnstn as agreed at first was that amendments might be prposed either by Cong or the legislatures. A commee was appointed to digest & redraw. Gov. Morris & [Rufus] King were of the commee. One morng Gov. M. moved an instrn for certain alterns (not 1/2 the members yet come in); in a hurry & without understanding it was agreed to. The commee reported so that Congr shld have the exclusive power of proposg amendmts. G. Mason observd it on the report & opposed it. King denied the constrn. Mason demonstrated it, & asked the commee by what authority they had varied what had been agreed. G. Morris then impudently got up & said by authority of the convention & produced the blind instruction beforementd, which was unknown by 1/2 of the house & not till then understood by the other. They then restored it as it stood originally." Farrand, vol. 3, pp. 367-68.

21. Poore, vol. 1, p. 257.

22. Ibid., p. 817.

23. See, for example, the 1777 constitution of Georgia, ibid., p. 377.

24. Ibid., vol. 2, pp. 1908-09.

25. Ibid., vol. 1, pp. 257, 32, 102, 195.

26. Ibid., pp. 278, 828.

27. Ibid., p. 383.

28. Ibid., p. 972. A provision for review in a particular year, or every so many years, was adopted by several states, but rarely was this instruction followed.

29. Ibid., vol. 2, p. 1548. This procedure apparently was not used by Pennsylvania, but when the new state of Vermont incorporated

a similar provision into its constitution, it followed the prescribed procedure to initiate amendments that were adopted in 1828, 1836, 1850, and 1870 (ibid., pp. 1883-87).

30. Ibid., pp. 1912-37.

31. Merrill D. Peterson, Democracy, Liberty and Property: The State Constitutional Conventions of the 1820's, pp. 137, 214-33. Peterson's documentary history and analysis of the conventions held by Massachusetts in 1820-21, New York in 1821, and Virginia in 1829-30 reveals most graphically the basic conflicts that beset American society in these early years.

32. Ibid., p. 434.

33. Ibid., p. 433.

34. Poore, vol. 1, pp. 278, 384, 388; vol. 2, pp. 1280, 1620, 1628.

35. The first constitutions of Vermont, admitted to the Union in 1791, Kentucky in 1792, Tennessee in 1796, Ohio in 1803, Louisiana in 1812, Indiana in 1816, Mississippi in 1817, Illinois in 1818, and Alabama in 1819, appear alphabetically, ibid., vol. 1, pp. 32-34, 439-46, 499-508, 647-56, 700-10; vol. 2, pp. 1054-64, 1455-64, 1667-76, 1858-65.

36. Ibid., vol. 1, pp. 30, 436-37, 497-98, 609; vol. 2, pp. 1453-54.

37. See, for example, the enabling acts for Colorado, Minnesota, and Nevada, ibid., vol. 1, p. 217; vol. 2, pp. 1027-28, 1245.

38. Ames, p. 282.

39. Ibid., p. 282.

40. Ibid., p. 282.

41. Ibid., p. 283.

42. Ibid., p. 285.

43. M. A. Musmanno, Proposed Amendments to the Constitution, pp. 189, 193.

44. Ames, p. 293. Rarely was any effort made to increase the difficulty of amendment. An exception was Rhode Island's attempt to introduce, concurrently with its reluctant ratification of the Constitution, a proposal that after 1793 no amendment could be approved "without the consent of eleven of the states heretofore united under the Confederation" (ibid., p. 292). Following this unsuccessful effort, 70 years passed before any further amendments to Article V were submitted to Congress.

45. Ibid., p. 293.

46. Ibid., pp. 293-94.

47. Musmanno, Proposed Amendments to the Constitution, p. 195.

48. Ibid., p. 197.

49. Ibid., p. 193.

50. Council of State Governments, "Amending the Constitution to Strengthen the States in the Federal System," State Government 36 (Winter 1963): 10-15. For an assessment of the council's proposals see Charles L. Black, Jr., "The Proposed Amendment of Article V: A Threatened Disaster," Yale Law Journal 72 (April 1963): 957-66.

51. Quoted by Representative Henry J. Hyde when he introduced his "Federal Constitutional Convention Amendment Act," CR (daily), 10 May 1977, p. H4260. For an understanding of the context in which Lincoln's remarks were made, see The Collected Works of Abraham Lincoln, ed. Roy P. Basler, vol. 4, p. 270.

52. A reported printed in CR (daily), 2 November 1977, p. S18494, put the total number of petitions at 374 as of September 1977, with 191 of these submitted subsequent to 1957.

53. James Stasny, "Toward a Critically Militant Electorate: A National Constitutional Convention," CR, vol. 122 (1976), p. 8985.

54. Ames, p. 285.

55. Lester B. Orfield, The Amending of the Federal Constitution, p. 43.

56. A tabulation by states and subjects of applications submitted from 1789 to 1973 is contained in ABA, appendix B. The 356 applications accounted for in this table do not include dozens submitted after 1973 on subjects like equal rights, abortion, school busing, and budget control.

# 2

## THE PROBLEM IN 1787

PRELUDE TO PHILADELPHIA

The constitutional convention that met in 1787 was the product of more than a decade of experience with a central government represented only by a unicameral legislature that had few enforceable powers and in which decisions were made on a one-state, one-vote basis. In its first year of operation, the Congress acted principally as a coordinator of grievances against the acts of Great Britain's king and parliament. After King George III officially declared the colonies to be in rebellion, Congress became the center from which revolutionary action was directed. [1]

During the first years of the Congress there was much talk of confederation, and specific plans were offered by three different Pennsylvania delegates: Joseph Galloway in 1774, Benjamin Franklin in 1775, and John Dickinson in 1776. Initially, however, independence was not the goal. In his "Plan of a Proposed Union between Great Britain and the Colonies," Galloway expressly denied any desire to separate from the mother country. [2] Rather, he advocated a "British and American legislature" that would join the colonies and Great Britain in a cooperative administration, much as Franklin had suggested 20 years earlier in his Albany Plan of Union. [3] Dickinson also was a vigorous opponent of political separation up to the point at which Congress foreclosed further debate on the matter by voting for a declaration of independence. Once that die had been cast, Dickinson joined in the preparation of one of the earliest drafts of the Articles of Confederation. [4] Even in this first effort to design a constitution that would formally unite the 13 states, many leaders in and out of Congress resisted any plan that would transfer essential elements of sovereignty from the states to a central authority. Early in 1776 Samuel Ward of Rhode Island and Samuel Adams of Massachusetts likened the resisters to the "dull horse" in one of Ward's favorite anecdotes. Ward wrote: "You may recollect the fable of the strong spirited horse and the lean one. . . . We are eternally plagued with that dull horse, sometimes he pricks up his ears and goes a little way and with spirit, then flaggs and is a dead weight upon his mate."[5] In Adams's view, had the spirited horse been in control of the Congress, "you would have seen that Confederation completed long before this time."[6] When finally the Articles of Confederation were approved by Congress more than a year after the Declaration of Independence, the strength of the demand for continuing local autonomy was evident in the description of the pact as "a firm league of friendship" in which "each state retains its sovereignty, freedom and independence, and every power, jurisdiction and right, which is not by this confederation expressly delegated to the United States in Congress assembled."[7]

The defects of this cautious approach to unified government were clear from the start, but facing up to the problem of political reorganization had to wait until peace had been gained and independence confirmed by the 1783 treaty with Great Britain. Even then, progress toward a stronger central government was slow. The Articles' provision that no modification of the compact could be made except by the unanimous agreement of all 13 states raised an almost impossible barrier to amendments. When in 1786 a few states attempted to attack one of the major problems—lack of coordinated control of foreign and interstate commerce—only Delaware, New Jersey, New York, Pennsylvania, and Virginia responded to the invitation to send representatives to a convention in Annapolis. Although the failure of a majority of states to participate in this meeting precluded any resolution of the problems for which the convention had been called, the assembled delegates did formally agree that the difficulty of amending the Articles of Confederation made it essential to consider a complete revision of that compact. The view expressed in their final report was that a new convention be called "to devise such further provisions as . . . to render the constitution of the Federal Government adequate to the exigencies of the Union." To insure the widest possible circulation of this recommendation, the delegates sent copies of the report not only to their own state legislatures, but also to "the United States in Congress assembled, and to the executives of the other states."[8]

The precarious condition of the country, as measured in its commercial, financial, and foreign relations, led a substantial majority of Congress to agree with the conclusion reached at Annapolis. Accordingly, Congress issued an invitation to all states to join in a convention in Philadelphia in 1787. Its letter of invitation used essentially the same justifying language as that contained in the Annapolis report. Twelve of the thirteen states (Rhode Island abstaining) sent delegates. As the smallest of the states, Rhode Island feared the curtailment of its freedom of action that was certain to follow from the adoption of any system having a strong central government. This fear was well founded, as the obvious intent of those leading the movement for revision of the Articles of Confederation was to overhaul the entire system and create a federal government with substantially increased authority. Some of the strongest supporters of the revolution, such as Samuel Adams and Patrick Henry, looked askance at efforts to form a strong national government, preferring a federation that would leave the states free of all but the most essential powers needed for defense and recognition in the international community.

That the broad purposes of the convention were recognized by the state legislatures when they approved sending delegations to Philadelphia is evident from their authorizing resolutions. Ten of the twelve used language identical or nearly identical to that of Congress, whose recommendation was that a convention be called, not just "for the sole and express purpose of revising the Articles of Confederation," but to design "such alterations and provisions therein as shall . . . render the federal constitution adequate to the exigencies of government and the preservation of the Union."[9] Only Delaware, which used a similar phrase, added a reservation that the Articles of Confederation principle of one-state, one-vote be retained.[10] Thus, although many delegates came to Philadelphia with either instructions or personal commitments to preserve some element of state sovereignty, this first effort at constitutional change was authorized with no formal limits on the nature or extent of modifications the convention might propose. Further, although the resolution of Congress referred to the Articles of Confederation as the source of authority for making alterations in that document, it did not cite, and the convention did not abide by, the procedures required by the Articles for effecting such changes. On the contrary, as Gouverneur Morris pointed out in a discussion of how the new constitution was to be ratified, "Mr. Elseworth [sic] erroneously supposes that we are proceeding on the basis of the Confederation. This convention is unknown to the Confederation."[11]


## THE CONVENTION'S FRAME OF REFERENCE

The precedent established in 1787 is still offered as an argument for the use of a national convention to initiate constitutional changes.

It is therefore important to consider the nature of the 1787 gathering and its relevance to twentieth-century politics.

First, as to the composition of the Philadelphia convention, one must remember that every delegate was selected by his (never her) state legislature; none was elected by popular vote. The state legislators themselves were chosen by an electorate that in most cases was limited to male landowners, or "freeholders." Convention discussion of the suffrage question as it applied to national elections clearly indicates the distrust most delegates felt for the judgment of landless persons. Women and slaves, of course, were not considered worthy of discussion at all, except in terms of the formula proposed to be used as the basis for representation. James Madison, who was far from the most conservative member of the convention, expressed a common concern when he said:

> Viewing the subject in its merits alone, the freeholders of the country would be the safest depositories of Republican liberty. In future times a great majority of the people will not only be without landed, but any other sort of, property. These will either combine under the influence of their common situation; in which case, the rights of property and the public liberty, will not be secure in their hands; or what is more probable, they will become the tools of opulence and ambition, in which case there will be equal danger on another side. [12]

Although the case for a wider suffrage base was argued by some delegates, the consensus was that the matter should be left to the states to decide on a local basis. This position was not altered when the convention reached the question of how the new constitution was to be ratified.

Compared to the extensive coverage given other items on the agenda at Philadelphia, relatively little time was spent on the method of ratifying the constitution, and even less on subsequent amendment procedures. Of the several outlines of proposed constitutions submitted by Edmund Randolph of Virginia, Charles Pinckney of South Carolina, William Patterson of New Jersey, and Alexander Hamilton of New York, only Randolph's referred directly to the method by which states would ratify the proposed constitution. [13] His suggestion was that, after approval by Congress, the constitution be submitted to "an assembly or assemblies of representatives recommended by the several [state] legislatures, to be expressly chosen by the people." [14] This proposal provided the starting point for discussion that centered about two problems: the number of state ratifications required to

bring the new constitution into effect, and whether ratification should
be by state legislatures or by specially elected state conventions.

On the first point, suggestions ranged from a simple majority
of seven of the thirteen states to unanimous approval by all. Those
advocating a strong central government were more inclined to accept
seven, eight, or nine ratifications as sufficient; those who desired
to see the maximum autonomy retained by the states argued for a
minimum of ten approvals. Daniel Carroll of Maryland fought strenu-
ously for a requirement that all 13 states ratify, but when this was
put to a ballot only Maryland voted for it. [15] The number finally
agreed upon was nine, which had been required by the Articles of
Confederation for decisions on major questions relating to war and
peace, treaties, coinage, and appropriations.

More vociferous and prolonged was the debate over whether
ratification should be by state legislatures or newly elected conventions. In general, supporters of adoption by nine or fewer states led
the argument in favor of ratification by conventions. Delegates who
had held out for adoption by ten or more states tended to favor ratification by state legislatures. Edmund Randolph's Virginia colleagues,
James Madison and George Mason, supported his proposal for ratification by conventions, pointing out that to rely on state legislatures
would bypass "the supreme authority of the people," and would subject the plan for national government to state tribunals of doubtful
authority and having a narrow view that would be expressed by "local
demagogues" interested principally in protecting their own power.
Opponents of the convention plan focused on the Articles of Confederation provision for ratification by state legislatures and the danger
of leaving decisions of such importance to the people. Elbridge Gerry
announced that in his state of Massachusetts, the people "have at
this time the wildest ideas of government in the world." [16] They were
divided, he said, into two parties, "one devoted to Democracy, the
worst . . . of all political evils, the other as violent in the opposite
extreme." [17] Gerry believed only confusion would come from referring the constitution to the people, who would not be able to agree on
anything. Although some of the most persistent defenders of ratification by state legislatures were from Massachusetts, Connecticut,
and Pennsylvania, when a proposal to this effect was put to a vote,
their delegations opposed it. In the end, a resolution for ratification
by conventions carried with no negative votes. [18]

On the procedure for amending the new constitution, the delegates sometimes divided along very different lines. Charles Pinckney
"doubted the propriety or necessity" of an amendment clause. Gerry,
who led the fight for states' rights, initially favored such a provision
because "the novelty and difficulty of the experiment requires peri-

odical revision. "[19] However, as discussion moved to the details of
procedural design, Gerry opposed almost every suggestion that would
permit amendment without the unanimous consent of all states. He
argued against initiation of amendments by a convention called at the
request of two-thirds of the states, declaring that in such an arrangement a majority of the convention could "bind the Union to innovations
that may subvert State Constitutions altogether. "[20] Gerry's attack
initiated a movement to reverse an earlier decision on this point, for
until the last week of the four-month debate, the convention method
of proposing amendments was the only one considered. When Roger
Sherman and Gerry were joined by Hamilton and Madison in an attempt to substitute Congress as the initiating agency, Mason and
Randolph led the counterattack and forced a compromise that provided
for the use of either method. [21]

Once the basic formula had been decided, only two reservations
were added. One was proposed by John Rutledge of South Carolina,
who won acceptance of a statement that would protect slaveholding
states against any amendment affecting that institution until 1808. [22]
The second was a motion by Gouverneur Morris, who gained approval
of a proviso that "no state, without its consent shall be deprived of
its equal suffrage in the Senate. "[23] This last, seemingly ironclad,
protection for small states undoubtedly helped bring the absent Rhode
Island into the fold when the constitution was presented to the states
for ratification. But the new amendment procedure, though difficult
to apply in practice, was far less stringent than that required by the
Articles of Confederation.

On the whole, adoption of Article V was achieved with less
bitter debate than was aroused by many other sections of the Constitution. The strongest objections came from the only three delegates
who, for different reasons, refused to sign the completed document:
Randolph and Mason of Virginia, and Gerry of Massachusetts. In
addition to the arguments of these delegates cited earlier, Randolph
believed that two of the most serious defects of the proposed system
were reflected in the convention's refusal to permit states to offer
amendments to the constitution that would be sent to them for approval,
or to hold another national convention to pass upon the states' suggested changes. [24] However, neither of these objections was among
the 20 reservations that Virginia included in its instrument of ratification. [25] Like the reservations of many other states, those of Virginia focused on areas in which federal power should be restricted,
and the most important of the proposed modifications were quickly
added to the Constitution as the first ten amendments.

As farsighted as some of the Philadelphia delegates were, they
could not have anticipated the bitterness of modern-day wrangling
over their intentions in two vital areas: the limits (if any) that may be

placed upon conventions called to modify the Constitution under
Article V, and the role of the president (if any) in the amendment
process. Because these two problems are at the core of current debates over the calling of a convention, a more intensive look at the
origins of the amendment process is necessary.

The first and most critical question is whether or not a constitutional convention can be limited in the subjects it considers or the
recommendations it makes, either by Congress or by the petitions
Congress receives from state legislatures requesting that a convention be called. Present-day answers to this question range from an
unequivocal no to an equally adamant yes. The two extremes were
expressed in testimony offered by witnesses at a 1967 Senate committee hearing on a bill introduced by Senator Sam Ervin of North Carolina to establish controls over the calling and functioning of a federal
constitutional convention.[26] On the negative side, Senator Joseph D.
Tydings of Maryland provided the most forceful statement in recalling
an opinion voiced in the Senate early in the twentieth century:

> When the people of the United States meet in a constitu-
> tional convention there is no power to limit their action.
> They are greater than the Constitution. They can repeal
> the provision that limits the right of amendment: they
> can repeal every section of it because they are the peers
> of the people who made it.[27]

The opposite view was presented by Professor Wallace Mendelson,
who argued as follows:

> Can a constitutional convention be limited? I think it can.
> I think it should. The convention of 1787 was. It sent its
> proposal to the Congress not merely for transmittal to
> the States but for approval by the Congress and then
> transmittal to the States. Such a "request" for approval
> by the Congress would seem to imply that Congress was
> free to disapprove. . . . The reason for including the
> convention system in article V seems to have been per-
> fectly clear to provide a means for correcting errors;
> that is, specific, concrete errors or abuses by the
> National Government.[28]

What is "perfectly clear" about the general purpose of Article V,
unfortunately, is not at all clear as to the more specific question of
whether or not the scope of convention authority may be limited. The
difficulty of determining the framers' intent on this point is evident
from the following detailed examination of the evolution of Article V.

ARTICLE V: THE DEBATE

Substantive discussion of constitutional matters by delegates to the Philadelphia convention of 1787 began with consideration of the Virginia Plan submitted by Edmund Randolph on May 29.[29] On the subject of amendment, that plan suggested only that "provision ought to be made for the amendment of the Articles of Union whensoever it shall seem necessary, and that the assent of the National Legislature ought not to be required thereto."[30] When the convention first reached this part of Randolph's proposals, the matter was postponed after only brief comments by Charles Pinckney of South Carolina, who "doubted the propriety or necessity of it," and Elbridge Gerry of Massachusetts, who offered the following in favor of the resolution:

> The novelty and difficulty of the experiment requires periodical revision. The prospect of such a revision would also give intermediate stability to the Govt. Nothing had yet happened in the States where this provision existed to prove its impropriety.[31]

A week later the convention deferred consideration of the provision that would exclude action by the national legislature, but approved the rest of the clause after another brief exchange reported in James Madison's notes as follows:

> Several members did not see the necessity of the resolution at all, nor the propriety of making the consent of the National Legislature unnecessary.
>
> Col. Mason urged the necessity of such a provision. The plan now to be formed will certainly be defective, as the Confederation has been found on trial to be. Amendments therefore will be necessary, and it will be better to provide for them, in an easy, regular and Constitutional way than to trust to chance and violence. It would be improper to require the consent of the Natl. Legislature, because they may abuse their power, and refuse their consent on that very account. The opportunity for such an abuse, may be the fault of the Constitution calling for amendmt.
>
> Mr. Randolph enforced these arguments.[32]

The first report of the Committee of the Whole on the entire Virginia Plan simply repeated the previously approved clause "that provision ought to be made for the amendment of the Articles of Union whensoever it shall seem necessary."[33] This wording was again approved by the convention without debate.[34] It remained in the same form when the collected decisions of the convention, taken over the first two months of deliberation, were referred to a Committee of Detail for review and refinement.

The committee responsible for editing the convention's early work was made up of delegates representing different geographic areas and interests, as well as different concepts of central government organization and powers. Its members were John Rutledge of South Carolina (chairman), Edmund Randolph of Virginia, Nathaniel Gorham of Massachusetts, Oliver Ellsworth of Connecticut, and James Wilson of Pennsylvania.[35] Historian Max Farrand refers to Wilson as "an important member of the committee,"[36] and, indeed, several of the committee drafts have been found to be in Wilson's handwriting. It is also true, however, that the Wilson drafts and one of those penned by Randolph contain essentially the same wording on amendment procedure.[37] Notwithstanding their differences on many issues, the members of this committee combined to produce a report that included a number of substantive changes in sections of the constitution previously adopted by the whole convention. The amendment provision is a case in point: in place of a simple acknowledgment of the need to provide for modification of the constitution, the committee devised the following specific procedure:

> On the application of the legislatures of two thirds of the States in the Union, for an amendment of this Constitution, the Legislature of the United States shall call a convention for that purpose.[38]

The committee's full report was submitted to the convention on August 6, but the amendment section was not reached for discussion until September 10, only a week before the convention finished its work. At that point the matter of amendment procedure was subjected to the first of only two debates in which the give-and-take involved more than brief comment by two or three delegates. Gerry began the discussion by asking that the article be reconsidered because of its possible impact on state constitutions. The following exchange of views is reproduced in full from Madison's notes.[39]

> This Constitution he [Gerry] said is to be paramount to the State Constitutions. It follows, hence, from this article that two thirds of the States may obtain a convention, a majority of which can bind the Union to innovations that may subvert the State-Constitutions altogether. He asked whether this was a situation proper to be run into.

Mr. Hamilton 2ded the motion, but he said with a different view from Mr. Gerry. He did not object to the consequence stated by Mr. Gerry. There was no greater evil in subjecting the people of the U.S. to the major voice than the people of a particular State. It had been wished by many and was much to have been desired that an easier mode for introducing amendments had been provided by the Articles of Confederation. It was equally desireable now that an easy mode should be established for supplying defects which will probably appear in the new system. The mode proposed was not adequate. The State Legislatures will not apply for alterations but with a view to increase their own powers. The National Legislature will be the first to perceive and will be most sensible to the necessity of amendments, and ought also to be empowered, whenever two thirds of each branch should concur to call a Convention. There could be no danger in giving this power, as the people would finally decide in the case.

Mr. Madison remarked on the vagueness of the terms, "call a Convention for the purpose," as sufficient reason for reconsidering the article. How was a convention to be formed? by what rule decide? what the force of its acts?

[At this point Gerry's motion to reconsider was approved.]

Mr. Sherman moved to add to the article "or the Legislature may propose amendments to the several States for their approbation, but no amendments shall be binding until consented to by the several States."

Mr. Gerry 2ded the motion.

Mr. Wilson moved to insert "two thirds of" before the words "several States." . . . [Motion defeated.]

Mr. Wilson then moved to insert "three fourths of" before "the several Sts" which was agreed to nem. con.

Mr. Madison moved to postpone the consideration of the amended proposition in order to take up the following.

"The Legislature of the U.S. whenever two thirds of both Houses shall deem necessary, or on the application of two thirds of the Legislatures of the several States, shall propose amendments to this Constitution, which shall be valid to all intents and purposes as part thereof, when the same shall have been ratified by three fourths at least of the Legislatures of the several States, or by Conventions in three fourths thereof, as one or the other mode of ratification may be proposed by the Legislature of the U.S."

Mr. Hamilton 2ded the motion.

Mr. Rutlidge [sic] said he never could agree to give a power by which the articles relating to slaves might be altered by the States not interested in that property and prejudiced against it. In order to obviate this objection these words were added to the proposition: "provided that no amendments which may be made prior to the year 1808, shall in many manner affect the 4 & 5 sections of the VII article"—The postponement being agreed to,

On the question of the proposition of Mr. Madison & Mr. Hamilton as amended [approved].

At the conclusion of debate on September 10, a Committee of Style and Arrangement was assigned the task of putting the constitutional document into final form. This committee was made up of William Samuel Johnson of Connecticut (chairman), Alexander Hamilton of New York, Gouverneur Morris of Pennsylvania, James Madison of Virginia, and Rufus King of Massachusetts,[40] a group more uniformly supportive of strong central government than the earlier Committee of Detail. Copies of the committee's report were circulated to convention delegates September 12. A final review of the finished document occurred September 15, the day on which the full Constitution was approved by the convention. On that occasion the following exchange dealt with what had by then become Article V:[41]

Mr. Sherman expressed his fears that three fourths of the States might be brought to do things fatal to particular States, as abolishing them altogether or depriving them of their equality in the Senate. He thought it reasonable that the proviso in favor of the States importing slaves should be extended so as to provide that no State should be affected in its internal police, or deprived of its equality in the Senate.

Col. Mason thought the plan of amending the Constitution exceptionable & dangerous. As the proposing of amendments is in both the modes to depend, in the first immediately, in the second, ultimately, on Congress, no amendments of the proper kind would ever be obtained by the people, if the Government should become oppressive, as he verily believed would be the case.[42]

Mr. Govr. Morris & Mr. Gerry moved to amend the article so as to require a convention on application of 2/3 of the Sts.

Mr. Madison did not see why Congress would not be
as much bound to propose amendments applied for by two
thirds of the States as to call a convention on the like application. He saw no objection however against providing
for a convention for the purpose of amendments, except
only that difficulties might arise as to the form, the
quorum, etc. which in constitutional regulations ought to
be as much as possible avoided.

The motion of Mr. Govr. Morris & Mr. Gerry was
agreed to nem. con.

Mr. Sherman moved to strike out of art. V. after
"legislatures" the words "of three fourths" and so after
the word "Conventions" leaving future conventions to act
in this matter, like the present convention according to
circumstances. [Defeated]

Mr. Gerry moved to strike out the words "or by Conventions in three fourths thereof." [Defeated]

Mr. Sherman moved according to his idea above
expressed to annex to the end of the article a further
proviso "that no State shall without its consent be affected
in its internal police, or deprived of its equal suffrage
in the Senate."

Mr. Madison. Begin with these special provisos, and
every State will insist on them, for their boundaries,
exports, &c.

[Sherman's motion defeated]

Mr. Sherman then moved to strike out art V altogether.
Mr. Brearley 2ded the motion. [Defeated]

Mr. Govr. Morris moved to annex a further proviso—
"that no State, without its consent shall be deprived of
its equal suffrage in the Senate."

This motion being dictated by the circulating murmurs
of the small States was agreed to without debate, no one
opposing it, or on the question, saying no.

Revealing as these discussions may be as to the fears of small
states, or the mutual distrust of the supporters of amendment initiation by Congress on the one hand and by convention on the other,
they offer no basis for a firm conclusion as to the delegates' intent
with respect to the scope of authority a national convention would
have. Only Madison commented on some of the problems a convention
would face, but the question of limited versus unlimited authority was
not one of them. No other delegate raised this specific question or
pursued the problems referred to by Madison. Gerry's reference to
"periodical revision" might reasonably be interpreted as anticipating

an occasional reevaluation of the entire Constitution. The remarks of Rutledge about slavery, and those of Sherman regarding amendments that might abolish states or deprive them of equality in the Senate, suggest their belief that each problem could be attacked separately. The Committee of Detail's use of "an amendment" and "that purpose"—both in the singular—suggests that the amendment process was expected to be used principally for modifying individual segments of the Constitution as each demonstrated a particular weakness. But the grammatical construction of the phrase does not necessarily imply an intent that each such convention should be limited to consideration of one or more specific problems. Nor can the reverse be inferred from later versions of Article V that permit either Congress or a convention to "propose amendments"—in the plural.

Moving on to the debates held in state conventions called to ratify the Constitution, one finds that the two greatest concerns of those opposed to ratification were the threat to state authority and the absence of a bill of rights. As a result, a major question in many state conventions was whether to give "conditional approval," subject to acceptance of their proposed amendments, or to ratify in anticipation that the amendments would be approved subsequently. The amendment procedure itself was mentioned only occasionally. Patrick Henry, one of the most bitter critics of the Philadelphia convention's work, insisted that Article V made amendments impossible because "To suppose that so large a number as three fourths of the states will concur is to suppose that they will possess genius, intelligence, and integrity, approaching to miraculous."[43] Responding to this view, Wilson Nicholas told the Virginia convention that he favored Article V, including the convention system, which he preferred for these reasons:

> The conventions which shall be so called will have their deliberations confined to a few points; no local interest to divert their attention; nothing but the necessary alterations. They will have many advantages over the last convention. No experiments to devise; the general and fundamental regulations being already laid down.[44]

The position of Nicholas probably comes as close to the concept of a limited convention as any expressed during this formative period. But Nicholas had no part in drafting the Constitution. His Virginia colleague, James Madison, made no attempt to resolve this question. In postconvention comments directed specifically to Article V, Madison limited his remarks to a relatively brief justification of that section as a whole.[45] Only when dealing with the proposed federal structure did he (and Hamilton) return to the convention issue, indicating distrust of any "appeal to the people" through conventions called to consider constitutional questions. However, when a "general convention" was proposed as a means of initiating the dozen or more amendments sought by many states at the time of ratification, Madison's opposition to this procedure reflected the same fear of an all-out attack on the Constitution that pervades Congress today.[46]

In their joint effort to secure ratification, Madison and Hamilton took pains to rebut the argument that changes in the Constitution, demanded by some as the price of ratification, should be made before adoption rather than after. Commenting on a proposal in the New York convention that ratification be accompanied by a reservation permitting rescission of that state's approval if desired amendments were not made, Madison wrote:

> My opinion is that a reservation of a right to withdraw if amendments be not decided on under the form of the Constitution within a certain time, is a conditional ratification, that it does not make N. York a member of the New Union, and consequently that she could not be received on that plan. Compacts must be reciprocal, this principle would not in such a case be preserved. The Constitution requires an adoption in toto, and for ever. It has been so adopted by the other States. An adoption for a limited time would be as defective as an adoption of some of the articles only. In short any condition whatever must viciate [sic] the ratification[47] [Madison's emphasis].

Hamilton concurred in this view, but he went further than Madison in his postconvention discussion of Article V. His concluding appeal to the public in the series of articles written with Madison and Jay included the following paragraph:

> But every amendment to the Constitution, if once established, would be a single proposition, and might be brought forward singly. There would then be no necessity for management or compromise, in relation to any other point—no giving nor taking. The will of the requisite number would at once bring the matter to a decisive issue. And consequently, whenever nine, or rather ten States, were united in the desire of a particular amendment that amendment must infallibly take place. There can, therefore, be no comparison between the facility of affecting an amendment and that of establishing in the first instance a complete Constitution.[48]

Although Hamilton's distinction between the objectives of the Philadelphia convention and those of subsequent conventions called to amend the Constitution implies acceptance of the limited convention concept, his immediate purpose was not to deal with that question, but to convince New York voters that it made more sense to adopt the proposed Constitution and amend it later, if necessary, rather than attempt to arrive at a perfect document before accepting any new constitution. This matter was argued at length by many political leaders of the time, but in none of the convention or postconvention literature does one find reference to the specific problem of the powers a future convention should have.[49]

In short, during the formative period of American constitutional history, the closest the country came to a direct confrontation on the question of a limited or an unlimited convention was in the discussions that preceded and led up to the Philadelphia convention. Neither the delegates to that assembly nor the leaders who subsequently debated acceptance of the convention's work faced this issue in their consideration of Article V.

## THE ROLE OF THE EXECUTIVE

An equally controversial, if less critical, question arises in connection with the impact of Article I, section 7 on the amendment process. As finally adopted by the Philadelphia convention, this portion of the Constitution included the following statement:

> Every order, resolution, or vote to which the concurrence of the Senate and House of Representatives may be necessary (except on a question of adjournment) shall be presented to the President of the United States; and before the same shall take effect, shall be approved by him, or, being disapproved by him, shall be repassed by two thirds of the Senate and House of Representatives, according to the rules and limitations prescribed in the case of a bill.[50]

This provision, which has remained unchanged since 1787, is the source of the argument that any congressional resolution relating to the establishment or control of a constitutional convention is subject to presidential approval or veto.

In reviewing the actions of the 1787 convention on this subject, one discovers that the role of the president in relation to the legislature generally was first considered in connection with proposals to establish an executive branch independent of Congress. Of the several

plans formally submitted to the convention, only the Virginia Plan
included a proposal for executive review of legislative acts. Neither
Paterson's nor Pinckney's plan contained such a provision. Hamilton's
"sketch" suggested an absolute executive veto, a view that received
some support although, as indicated earlier, Hamilton's package of
proposals was never taken up formally as a basis for discussion.

On the question of executive review of legislation, the convention took as its starting point a segment of the Virginia Plan that
read:

> Resd. that the Executive and a convenient number of the
> National Judiciary, ought to compose a Council of revision
> with authority to examine every act of the National Legis-
> lature before it shall operate, & every act of a particular
> Legislature before a negative thereon shall be final; and
> that the dissent of the said Council shall amount to a re-
> jection, unless the Act of the National Legislature be
> again negatived by [        ] of the members of each
> branch. [51]

When first considered as a separate item, this section was discussed as one aspect of the larger question of how the executive
branch should be constituted. In the course of several days of debate
on that broader subject, Elbridge Gerry suggested that the notion of
a council of revision was a poor one, particularly if it would give
members of the judiciary an opportunity to pass judgment on matters
of public policy before such matters reached the courts. He proposed
modifying Randolph's provision regarding an executive veto to read:
"The National Executive shall have a right to negative any legislative
act which shall not be afterward passed by [        ] parts of each
branch of the national Legislature."[52] Subsequent discussion of this
point focused on whether or not the veto should be absolute and, if
not, by what majority the legislature should be permitted to override
the executive. The several opinions advanced were clearly concerned
with the process of enacting ordinary legislation. There is not the
slightest hint that any delegate had in mind the more special function
of amending the Constitution. Near the close of this first debate on
the subject, agreement was reached to insert "two thirds" into the
blank space in Gerry's motion.[53] Six weeks later this provision was
again considered, and the executive's "right to negative legislative
acts not afterwards passed by 2/3 of each branch" was approved
without objection.[54] When, after a brief period, the notion of a council of revision was revived, debate centered about two aspects of the
problem: the doctrine of separation of powers, and the need to curtail
undesirable laws.[55]

After a number of matters had been discussed at some length, a summary of convention decisions that was referred to the Committee of Detail on July 26 included Gerry's proposed provision for an executive veto.[56] Records of that committee reveal that Randolph continued to think of the veto as an element of the executive function belonging in the executive section of the Constitution. A draft prepared by Wilson, on the other hand, suggested that the proper place for a description of the veto was in a section dealing with legislative functions.[57] The document the committee returned to the convention on August 6 reflected the committee's final agreement on a reorganization of material. This shifted the provision for executive review of legislation out of the article on the executive branch and into one of the several articles on the legislature.[58] The relevant section of this revised draft, which at this stage was part of Article VI, read as follows:

Sect. 13. Every bill, which shall have passed the House of Representatives and the Senate, shall, before it become a law, be presented to the President of the United States for his revision: if, upon such revision, he approve of it, he shall signify his approbation by signing it: But if, upon such revision, it shall appear to him improper for being passed into a law, he shall return it, together with his objections against it, to that House in which it shall have originated, who shall enter the objections at large on their journal and proceed to reconsider the bill. But if after such reconsideration, two thirds of that House shall, notwithstanding the objections of the President, agree to pass it, it shall together with his objections, be sent to the other House, by which it shall likewise be reconsidered, and if approved by two thirds of the other House also, it shall become a law.

As is evident throughout this section of the draft, the reference was to "a bill" that may or may not become "a law." There is no evidence to suggest that any member of the committee considered executive review as applying to the amendment process.

As the convention proceeded to consider the document prepared by the Committee of Detail, it concentrated first on Articles III through IX, all dealing with the legislative branch. Some delegates suggested that there was a difference between ordinary and special legislative functions, citing "balloting for appointments," approval of treaties, and "inquisitorial powers" as particular examples.[59] In these three cases, the subject of discussion was the relation between the House and Senate, not between the legislature and executive.

Executive-legislative relations were very much an issue, however, when appointment of ambassadors and the treaty power generally were considered.[60] There was also some talk of the legislature's right to decide upon adjournment and the location of the central government without interference from the executive.[61] But in none of these discussions was any reference made to the special conditions attending the amendment process.

Not until debate reached Article VI, section 13, was the executive's role in the legislative process considered at length.[62] Madison then moved that "all acts before they become laws should be submitted both to the Executive and Supreme Judiciary Departments, that if either of these should object 2/3 of each House, if both should object, 3/4 of each House, should be necessary to overrule the objections and give to the acts the force of law." As in earlier debates in this area, the issue was one of separation of powers, and the majority supported Roger Sherman's view that judges ought not to be "meddling in politics and parties." With this point settled, Madison called attention to the fact that if executive review were confined to "bills," the legislature could evade executive action "by acts under the form and name of resolution, votes, etc." He proposed that the phrase "or resolve" be added after "bill." But, in Madison's own words, "after a short and rather confused conversation on the subject, the question was put and rejected." The confusion appears to have been dispelled by the following day, for when Randolph then offered essentially the same proposal as Madison's, it was approved with only one state opposed. Randolph's motion read:

> Every order [,] resolution or vote, to which the concurrence of the Senate & House of Reps. may be necessary (except on a question of adjournment and in the cases hereinafter mentioned) shall be presented to the President for his revision; and before the same shall have force shall be approved by him, or being disapproved by him shall be repassed by the Senate & House of Reps. according to the rules & limitations prescribed in the case of a bill.

This action of August 16 remained uncontested for the remainder of the convention. When the final draft of the full Constitution was submitted by the Committee of Style and Arrangement on September 12, the only change in this section, other than editorial polishing, was the deletion of the phrase "and in cases hereinafter mentioned" from the parenthetical note that referred to matters excluded from presidential review.[63] Three days later the convention approved the completed Constitution without further modification of this paragraph. No explanation has been found for striking the open-ended phrase, "cases

hereinafter mentioned. " A reasonable inference is that the group preferred to mention only the one specific exclusion that had been agreed
upon, rather than leave the door open to later interpretations that
might expand the list to include items the convention would not have
approved.

It is precisely at this point that strict-constructionists argue
that in the absence of a specific exclusion of resolutions relating to
the amendment process, such actions must be submitted to the president. What this view fails to take into account is that all convention
discussions of executive veto turn about the problem of executive
interference with, or protection against, actions of the legislature
taken in the normal process of lawmaking. As Gouverneur Morris
said when the matter was raised for the second time, "Either bad
laws will be pushed or not. On the latter supposition no check will
be wanted. On the former a strong check will be necessary. . . ."[64]
He went on to describe the kinds of laws or interests that might lead
to bad legislation but, like others arguing this point, he did not even
hint that his fears included the possibility of a threat to the Constitution itself. Similarly, an examination of the records relating to
Article V reveals that none of the views expressed by delegates at
the convention suggests that the amendment process was ever considered related to Article I.

Nor did this situation change during the lengthy and heated
debates on ratification. In the extensive letter writing, pamphleteer-
ing, and speech making of late 1787 and 1788, arguments for and
against the proposed Constitution followed the same general pattern
as in the Philadelphia convention. Supporters cited the absolute
necessity of a government as structured in the Constitution and
defended each provision at length.[65] Detractors pointed to the illegality of the entire venture, which ignored the amendment provision of
the Articles of Confederation, decried the absence of a bill of rights,
and cited many objectionable elements in the new system, including
what were conceived as weaknesses in the design of the executive
branch.[66] But neither side referred to the president's role in the
amendment process. Even the most exhaustive examinations of the
Constitution, such as those in The Federalist essays and in Patrick
Henry's many hours of argument in the Virginia convention, ranged
over all aspects of the proposed executive-legislative relations without the slightest indication of a belief that the president would have a
role in any stage of the amendment process. At times, the analysis
ran in a contrary direction, as when several delegates to the North
Carolina convention protested the executive veto as "a legislative
power given to the President, and implies a contradiction to that part
[of the Constitution] which says that all legislative power is vested in
the two houses [of Congress]. "[67] Jonathan Elliot's historic collection

of documents relating to the debates over ratification includes "A Short History of the Veto," which refers repeatedly and exclusively to the effect of presidential action on "bills" and "laws."[68]

As in the case of convention authority, the evidence relating to the role of the president does not, in a positive sense, demonstrate an intent one way or the other. However, the answer to this question rests as much on what was not said in the 1787-88 debates as on the opinions that were expressed. Considered in this light, the negative evidence points overwhelmingly to the conclusion that Article I, section 7 was intended to apply only to those legislative functions referred to in other portions of that article and not to congressional actions taken under Article V. In the thousands of words and many months of argument devoted to the powers of the president, including his position vis-à-vis Congress, one can find no evidence that the specific question of his role in any aspect of the amendment process ever arose, either in connection with Article I or Article V. It is difficult to conceive of two constitutional issues—which strict-constructionists insist are related—being subjected to such close scrutiny by so great a variety of politically astute observers, for so long a period of time, without someone, somewhere, raising a question or making a comment about the effect of one procedure on the other. Hence, although in a literal sense one may argue that under Article I, section 7, "a resolution is a resolution is a resolution," and every act of Congress so identified must be subject to presidential approval, nothing in the formative history of Article I will support the application of this principle to actions taken under Article V. On the contrary, the very fact that the amendment process was, on every occasion, debated as a separate and distinct problem unrelated to other legislative functions, suggests that the intent was not to treat that process in the same way as matters requiring both legislative and executive action.

## NOTES

1. Some intimate glimpses of the people and politics of the American Revolution are offered by Library of Congress, Letters of Delegates to Congress 1774-1789. As of July 1980 only five volumes, covering the period August 1774 to December 1776, had been published. Among the earliest papers in volume 1 are selections from John Adams's diary that report the first formal meeting of Congress on 4 September 1774. King George's Proclamation of Rebellion was issued 23 August 1775, but news of this action did not reach the colonies until November 1 of that year.

2. Henry Steele Commager, ed., Documents of American History, 2d ed. (1940), pp. 81-82.

3. Ibid., pp. 43–45.

4. Dickinson's resistance to separation from Great Britain is clearly set forth in many of the Letters of Delegates to Congress (cited in note 1, above), vols. 1-4. For his draft of the Articles of Confederation, together with one by Josiah Bartlett of New Hampshire, see ibid., vol. 4, pp. 233-50.

5. Samuel Ward to Henry Ward, 8 January 1776, ibid., vol. 3, p. 61.

6. Samuel Adams to James Warren, 7 January 1776, ibid., pp. 52-53. Later, Adams had serious reservations about the Philadelphia convention's proposal for what he saw as "a national government instead of a federal union of sovereign states," but ultimately he supported the Massachusetts convention's resolution to ratify the Constitution. William V. Wells, The Life and Public Services of Samuel Adams, vol. 3, pp. 251-70.

7. Docs, p. 27. Although approved by Congress in 1777, the Articles of Confederation were not ratified by the last of the 13 states until 1781.

8. Ibid., p. 43. As the convention report noted, "commissioners" were appointed by New Hampshire, Massachusetts, Rhode Island, and North Carolina, but none of them attended. Connecticut, Maryland, South Carolina, and Georgia made no effort to participate.

9. Ibid., pp. 46, 55-84. For Madison's postconvention justification of this unlimited grant of authority see The Federalist, no. 40.

10. Docs, p. 67.

11. Ibid., p. 437. Madison acknowledges in The Federalist, nos. 40 and 43, that the convention and its proposals were not authorized by the Articles of Confederation, but he insisted that "absolute necessity" and "the great principle of self-preservation" made its actions essential.

12. Docs, pp. 489-90. This was a preview of the argument on the dangers of factionalism that Madison was to warn against in his later effort to secure popular support for the new constitution. See The Federalist, no. 10.

13. Docs, pp. 953-88 and Farrand, vol. 3, appendixes C, D, E, and F. Farrand notes that Philadelphia convention records refer to Pinckney's submission of a plan on May 29, but that no further reference appeared and no copy was ever found among convention documents. When these documents were prepared for publication in 1818, Pinckney submitted what he claimed was a draft of his original plan. Farrand reports that "King and Madison expressed privately their conviction that the document printed in the Journal [in 1819] was not the same as that originally presented by Pinckney in 1787" (ibid., pp. 601-2).

14. Docs, p. 119.

15. Ibid., p. 651.

16. Ibid., p. 156.

17. Ibid., p. 744.

18. Ibid., p. 735.

19. Ibid., p. 155.

20. Ibid., p. 695.

21. Ibid., p. 696. The details of this contest are included in a discussion of convention powers later in this chapter.

22. Ibid., pp. 696-97.

23. Ibid., p. 736.

24. Randolph detailed his objections in a report to the Virginia House of Delegates 10 October 1787. Farrand, vol. 3, pp. 123-27.

25. Docs, pp. 1027-34.

26. CC Hearings.

27. Ibid., p. 25. Quoted from a 1911 attack by Senator Weldon B. Heyburn of Idaho on the convention system and the then-proposed amendment for direct election of senators. CR 46: 2769-73.

28. CC Hearings, p. 45.

29. Docs, p. 116. Other proposals for a new constitution were introduced by William Patterson of New Jersey and Charles Pinckney of South Carolina (ibid., pp. 964-78). Alexander Hamilton outlined his plan orally but did not offer it formally for consideration (ibid., pp. 223-25, 979-88). Early in the convention's deliberations, a decision was made to use Randolph's proposals as the basis for discussion (ibid., p. 234).

30. Ibid., p. 119.

31. Ibid., p. 155.

32. Ibid., pp. 190-91.

33. Ibid., pp. 203, 234-37.

34. Ibid., p. 433.

35. Farrand, vol. 2, p. 97.

36. Ibid., vol. 1, p. xxii.

37. Ibid., vol. 2, pp. 137, 148, 157, 159.

38. Docs, p. 481.

39. Ibid., pp. 695-97.

40. Farrand, vol. 2, p. 547.

41. Docs, pp. 734-36.

42. Mason's view was more forcefully expressed in a marginal note he made on his copy of the committee report, in which he wrote that the revised article represented "a doctrine utterly subversive of the fundamental principles of the rights and liberties of the people." Farrand, vol. 2, p. 629, n. 8. For Mason's postconvention account of this development, see supra, Chapter 1, n. 20.

43. Jonathan Elliot, The Debates in the Several State Conven-

tions on the Adoption of the Federal Constitution as Recommended by the General Convention at Philadelphia in 1787, vol. 3, p. 49.

44. Ibid., p. 102. A more general defense of Article V was made by James Iredell in the North Carolina convention (ibid., vol. 4, pp. 176-77).

45. The Federalist, no. 43.

46. Ibid., nos. 49, 50. For Madison's comments on a "general convention" to amend the Constitution, see his letters of 8 April 1788 to George Nicholas and 2 January 1789 to George Eve in The Papers of James Madison, vol. 11, pp. 12-13, 404-5.

47. Madison to Hamilton, 20 July 1788, The Papers of Alexander Hamilton, vol. 5, pp. 184-85.

48. The Federalist, no. 85.

49. In addition to works previously cited, see: Jefferson's correspondence with John Adams, James Madison, and Uriah Forrest in The Papers of Thomas Jefferson, vol. 12, pp. 396, 438-42, 475-79; George Athan Billias, Elbridge Gerry, Founding Father and Republican Statesman, chap. 14; Charles Pinckney's "Observations on the Plan of Government Submitted to the Federal Convention in Philadelphia on the 28th of May, 1787," in Farrand, vol. 3, appendix CXXIX; Edmund Randolph's report of 10 October 1787 to the Virginia House of Delegates, ibid., appendix CXXXI; Luther Martin's address of 29 November 1787 to the Maryland House of Representatives, ibid., appendix CLVIII.

It is tempting to include here a reference to the character of amendment procedures adopted in the early state constitutions mentioned in Chapter 1. Although this would show substantial agreement on the use of either a convention or a poll of the electorate as one step in the amendment process, it cannot be shown to have had a bearing on the decisions or intentions of the delegates to the Philadelphia convention.

50. Docs, p. 705.
51. Ibid., p. 118.
52. Ibid., p. 147.
53. Ibid., p. 152.
54. Ibid., p. 400.
55. Ibid., pp. 422-29.
56. Ibid., pp. 465, 469.
57. Farrand, vol. 2, pp. 146, 167.
58. Docs, pp. 471, 474-75, 478-79.
59. Ibid., pp. 482-85.
60. Ibid., pp. 605-7, 683-86, 688-90.
61. Ibid., p. 521.
62. Ibid., pp. 547-52.

63. Ibid., p. 705.

64. Ibid., p. 425.

65. Comments on presidential powers made in the state conventions are indexed in Jonathan Elliot, Debates in the State Conventions. Additional sources include: The Federalist, nos. 51, 69, 73; The Papers of Thomas Jefferson, vol. 12, pp. 396, 440; Farrand, vol. 4, p. 81; Charles J. Stille, The Life and Times of John Dickinson, pp. 259-60; Max M. Mintz, Gouverneur Morris and the American Revolution, pp. 192-94.

66. See index references in Elliot, Debates in the State Conventions; Pinckney's "Observations" and Randolph's report, cited in note 29; newspaper articles from 1787-88 reproduced in Paul Leicester Ford, ed., Essays on the Constitution of the United States.

67. Elliot, Debates in the State Conventions, vol. 4, p. 27.

68. Ibid., pp. 620-24.

# 3

## THE SUPREME COURT ANSWERS
## SOME QUESTIONS

Of the thousands of amendments suggested in almost two hundred years of constitutional history, only 26 have been adopted. Ten of these might almost be considered part of the original Constitution, for they were demanded by many states in messages accompanying their resolutions ratifying the plan submitted to them in 1787, and were added to the Constitution within two years after it had gone into effect.

Like other elements of American law, the Constitution is subject to legal interpretation. The amendment procedures in Article V, although not the subject of litigation as frequently as many other parts of the Constitution, have been tested in the courts on a number of occasions. Of the cases that have reached the Supreme Court of the United States, few have had any direct bearing on the initiation of an amendment by a constitutional convention. Even without benefit of a previous confrontation on this issue, however, the problems that have been taken to the Supreme Court are worth examining for their implications in terms of questions that are bound to arise as demands for a constitutional convention approach the point of forcing a decision on the use of this method.

The effects of previous decisions can best be illustrated by the answers they provide to the following specific questions about the amendment process.

Q: Should the people of each state, as the "ultimate authority" in matters of public policy, have an opportunity to pass upon a proposed amendment to the United States Constitution?

A: Although the concept of popular sovereignty is basic to the American system of government, the federal Constitution provides for policymaking by elected representatives of the people rather than by the people directly. Only at state and local levels has this "republican" principle been broadened to permit the "democratic" process of decision making by direct action of the electorate in town meetings or referenda.

As applied to the amendment process, the question arose in two separate challenges to the Eighteenth Amendment (Prohibition), which involved attempts to subject the proposed constitutional change to state referenda. Both cases reached the Supreme Court in 1920. In considering the first challenge, which arose when Ohio attempted to implement a section of the state constitution that required a referendum to approve any amendment, the court pointed out that the federal Constitution makes no provision for action "by the people directly." At the state level, the court said, the federal Constitution assigns responsibility for decisions on proposed amendments to the "deliberative assemblages representative of the people."[1] Hence it found the provision in the Ohio constitution calling for a referendum inconsistent with Article V of the federal Constitution.

This judgment was confirmed a short time later when public and private agencies in seven states argued that "all sovereignty resides in the people," who must therefore be permitted a voice in any proposed change in the country's basic law. Plaintiffs pointed to the fact that the original Constitution was submitted for ratification to conventions chosen directly by the people of the 13 states then in the Union. The court held its ground, however, and insisted that "referendum provisions of state constitutions and statutes cannot be applied, consistently with the Constitution of the United States, in the ratification or rejection of amendments to it."[2]

From these decisions it is clear that the only road to direct public participation in the amendment process is by way of an amendment to Article V.[3] Even as applied to the ratification stage, the contention that popular sovereignty is appropriate under the existing terms of Article V rests on shaky ground when it assumes that the members of the 1787 convention intended to subject their work to direct action by all of the country's voters. As an argument for public participation in the initiation of amendments, the doctrine is far from the intentions of the founding fathers. In 1787, popular election of a national assembly to design a new constitution would have been considered by most political leaders to be not only impractical, but also extremely dangerous. The following decade would find such a notion applauded by many French revolutionaries, but the American objective of political independence did not envisage an uprooting of the entire social structure of society.

Q: What is the extent of congressional power to limit the
time allowed states for consideration of a proposed
amendment?

A: An important challenge to congressional authority arose when
Congress, for the first time, placed a limit on the time permitted for
ratification of an amendment. It did this when it forwarded the Eighteenth Amendment to the states with the stipulation that "This article
shall be inoperative unless it shall have been ratified as an amendment to the Constitution by the legislatures of the several States, as
provided in the Constitution, within seven years from the date of the
submission hereof to the States by the Congress." Opponents of the
proposal declared Congress had no right to add this proviso or any
other restriction on "what legislatures of the States shall do in their
deliberation."

When the protest reached the Supreme Court, that body held
that Article V "is intended to invest Congress with a wide range of
power in proposing amendments." It found this power to be limited
only in two ways specified in Article V: congressional approval must
be by two-thirds of both houses, and no amendment may be approved
that would deprive any state, without its consent, of equal representation in the Senate.[4] The court acknowledged that of 17 previously
adopted amendments, all had been ratified within four years, but it
pointed out that one unsuccessful amendment had been acted upon by
a state 80 years after its submission for ratification by Congress.
The court did not conjecture as to what its stand would have been
if approval by three-fourths of the states had been achieved only after
an 80-year lapse. But it did note that nothing in Article V suggests
"that an amendment once proposed is to be open to ratification for all
time." On the contrary, it observed that Article V treats the two
stages of proposal and ratification as "succeeding steps in a single
endeavor, the natural inference being that they are not to be widely
separated in time." In a rare example of indecision between the implications of the Constitution and the inferences to be drawn from it,
the court attempted to cover both approaches by concluding that "the
fair inference or implication from Article V is that ratification must
be within some reasonable time after the proposal."

Q: How many years constitute a "reasonable period of
time" for states to decide upon ratification of a proposed
amendment?

A: In holding that the time must be reasonable, the court has consistently refused to define that term. Rather, it has taken the position
that, in the absence of any reference to time in Article V, decisions

in that area must be made by Congress. When one plaintiff argued that Kansas had taken too long in ratifying the Child Labor Amendment 17 years after it had been proposed by Congress, the court refused either to confirm or deny the contention; it merely rejected plaintiff's plea that in the absence of a time limit set by Congress, the Supreme Court should decide what is a reasonable period.[5]

Since its first use in 1917, the seven-year period has become traditional for ratification. However, as later discussion will indicate, the time problem has been raised anew in connection with petitions for a constitutional convention.

Q: Having set a time limit for state approval of an amendment, may Congress subsequently alter that allowance?

A: This question first arose in connection with the Equal Rights Amendment when, after setting seven years as the limit for ratification, Congress voted to extend that period by an additional three years.[6] The extension was approved after a House committee had heard testimony from a number of expert witnesses, most of whom agreed that Congress had the power to extend the time allowance.[7] The right to reduce the number of years previously approved was challenged, but as this was not the immediate issue it was not given full consideration.

The action of Congress in extending the ERA ratification period has not been accepted by some state legislatures. Many of the ratifying resolutions submitted by states approving the amendment referred to the original deadline in such a way as to indicate the legislatures' belief—in some cases, their intent—that the amendment would become effective only if three-fourths of the states had ratified by that date. A clear demonstration of such intent was given by the South Dakota legislature when on 1 March 1979, three weeks before the original deadline, it resolved that its earlier approval would become "null and void" on 22 March 1979 if the required three-fourths of all states had not ratified the amendment by that time.[8] Two months later Arizona and Idaho joined in a suit asking the federal district court in Idaho to declare the extension of time unconstitutional. The far-reaching effects this action will have on both legal and legislative precedent are evident from the following concise summary of the complaint:

> The complaint prays for a declaratory judgment that the extension is unconstitutional and the Idaho rescission is valid. The complaint also asks for a mandatory injunction ordering the GSA [general services administrator] to return the resolutions of rescinding states and for a prohibiting injunction ordering the Administrator to deny recognition of any state approving ERA in the extension period.[9]

The decision to go to court in advance of actions by additional state legislatures was taken to avoid the possibility of ratification being declared by the general services administrator automatically upon receipt of the thirty-eighth approval, and regardless of rescissions by some of those 38 states. When this case reaches the Supreme Court, as it surely will, the court's established position that Congress has sole jurisdiction over amendment procedure will be put to a new test. The court will also be faced with a direct challenge to its earlier position on rescission, as discussion of the next question indicates.

Q: What is the effect of a state resolution to disapprove a proposed amendment, either before or after that state has voted to approve the same proposal?

A: Although posed as a single question because of the several related aspects of the problem covered by the Supreme Court in a key case, [10] it is essential to keep in mind the different conditions that may follow from congressional submission of an amendment to states for ratification. Consideration of the proposal by state legislatures may result in any one of the following: ratification; initial ratification followed by a later resolution to reject the amendment or to rescind the earlier approval; rejection; initial rejection followed by a subsequent resolution to ratify; no action either to approve or disapprove.

A number of proposed amendments initiated by Congress have long since been forgotten simply because they failed to get the approval of three-fourths of the states. In some cases more than one-fourth of the states voted against ratification; in others the proposal was never brought to a vote. Instances of disapproval or avoidance of the issue have, for the most part, generated little in the way of court action, even when a state has first rejected and subsequently approved an amendment. For example, the actions of Idaho and Texas in first rejecting and later ratifying the Twenty-second Amendment produced no litigation. However, a similar sequence of events in Kansas brought an appeal to the courts that led to a general review of this situation. The case arose out of a demand that Kansas officials be restrained from certifying that state's ratification of the Child Labor Amendment because of an earlier rejection by the legislature. In refusing to interfere with the certification, the Supreme Court did not actually weigh the effect of the prior rejection. It simply held that because Article V speaks only of ratification, there was no legal basis for disallowing that action.

Nor did the court have to face what has since become an even more explosive issue, as when a state first votes to ratify an amendment and later resolves to rescind its earlier action. Nevertheless, the court recognized this as a related problem and discussed it in terms of the history of the Fourteenth Amendment. When that modification of the Constitution was submitted to the states, Ohio and New Jersey first ratified the amendment and later passed resolutions withdrawing their consent. Despite the attempted withdrawals, the U.S. Secretary of State proclaimed ratification by the necessary three-fourths of the states and included Ohio and New Jersey in the list of approving states. Aware of the two reversals, Congress settled the issue by passing a concurrent resolution declaring the Fourteenth Amendment to be part of the Constitution by virtue of its approval by three-fourths of the states, including Ohio and New Jersey. The court's conclusion in 1939 was that "in accordance with this historic precedent the question of the efficacy of ratifications by state legislatures, in the light of previous rejection or attempted withdrawal, should be regarded as a political question pertaining to the political departments, with the ultimate authority in the Congress in the exercise of its control over the promulgation of the adoption of the amendment."

Interestingly enough, in leading up to its blanket acceptance of the precedent that only ratification actions can be recognized, the court acknowledged that some experts have challenged the view that a state legislature that has rejected an amendment may later ratify it. In the court's words, "The opposing view proceeds on the assumption that if ratifications by 'Conventions' were prescribed by the Congress, a convention could not reject and, having adjourned sine die, be reassembled and ratify." This being so, it is argued that the same reasoning should prevent approval by a state legislature after initial rejection on the ground that the state can act "but once, either by convention or through its legislature."

The extraordinary conditions surrounding the adoption of the Fourteenth Amendment—including initial rejection by some southern states that ratified the amendment after their post-Civil-War reorganization—are the basis for the Arizona-Idaho challenge to the Supreme Court's position in the Coleman case. In asking the court to declare its rescission of the Equal Rights Amendment valid, Idaho is seeking a reversal of the precedent that was established during a period in which "union military dictatorships" directed acceptance of the Fourteenth Amendment by states that had seceded as a precondition to renewal of their representation in Congress. Should this effort fail, and should a total of 38 state endorsements be recorded by the General Services Administrator, that officer will be obliged to announce and count all state approvals and disregard all resolutions of disapproval or rescission. If, when the Arizona-Idaho complaint reaches the nation's highest tribunal, the Supreme Court holds to its earlier position, it will be up to Congress to decide whether or not to accept the view that a state is entitled to withdraw an approval given earlier. This, no doubt, would lead to a suit by supporters of existing precedent, and the court would be asked to declare the action of Congress unconstitutional on the grounds that, in the court's own words: "Article V, speaking solely of ratification, contains no provisions as to rejections."

A different method of resolving this problem, which has been under consideration in Congress for over a decade, is discussed in Chapter 6.

Q: When does an amendment become effective as part of the Constitution?

A: For as long as the Supreme Court holds to its earlier position that negative responses to a proposed amendment are not recognized, the answer is simple: an amendment is considered ratified when affirmative responses have been received from three-fourths of the state legislatures. However, this answer assumes not merely that Congress may ignore negative responses, but that, more broadly, it has the authority to judge the acceptability of each response and to indicate when it is satisfied that constitutional requirements for ratification have been met. [11] Although for more than a century Congress has recognized only resolutions of approval, recent years have seen a growing demand for the right of state legislatures to alter their initial positions, either for or against ratification. The right to rescind a previous decision, discussed later in the context of legislation proposed to govern constitutional conventions, is likely to prove a major source of contention if and when such legislation comes up for consideration in a congressional committee or on the floor of either house.

Q: May states establish their own rules of procedure for approving proposed amendments?

A: State procedures must be consistent with Article V of the federal Constitution and any rules laid down by Congress under that article. As the Supreme Court has stated on several occasions, a state decision to hold a referendum on a proposed amendment would not be consistent with the provisions of Article V. From other positions taken by the court, it may also be assumed that a state may not depart from its normal legislative process in dealing with an amendment, though what is "normal" may not be the same in dealing with constitutional amendments as in treating ordinary legislation. The court might be expected to apply the same rule of normality to state actions as it has to the Congress in its decision that the two-thirds majority required in each house is calculated on the basis of "members present." However, the

court has shown that it cannot answer all questions in this area. For
example, in the Kansas petition that challenged the validity of that
state's ratification of the Child Labor Amendment because the deciding
vote was cast by the lieutenant governor, the court was evenly divided
on this point and so offered no opinion. [12]

Notwithstanding the court's position regarding the broad powers
accruing to the national legislature under Article V, Congress has
long been reluctant to lay down detailed rules for states to follow in
the amendment process. This reticence was demonstrated as far
back as 1866, when it was suggested that amendments initiated by the
national legislature be considered only by state legislatures elected
subsequent to the actions of Congress. Though unknown to federal
practice, the idea was reminiscent of a provision common to a number
of state constitutions. This provision required that after the legislature had initiated an amendment, it must inform the public of the
proposal by publication in newspapers statewide, after which the next
elected legislature would decide upon ratification. During debate on
the Fourteenth Amendment, Senator Charles R. Buckalew of Pennsylvania introduced a resolution to establish the following limitations on
the ratification procedure: the amendment could be considered only
by state legislatures chosen in the first election after the amendment
had been referred to the states by Congress; the decision for or
against ratification was to be taken at the first session of the new legislature; no subsequent session might reconsider the matter of acceptance or rejection; to be valid, ratifications had to be effected within
three years after congressional approval of the amendment. [13] These
restrictions were not accepted by the Senate; nor were similar conditions a number of senators endeavored to attach to the Fifteenth
Amendment. On the latter occasion, the cause of sincere believers
in procedural regulations for the ratification process was not advanced
by clear evidence that the proposed controls were part of "a system-
atic attempt to render its [the Fifteenth Amendment's] success
doubtful by endeavoring to secure its submission to the states for
ratification by some untried method. "[14] Nevertheless, arguments
offered in support of the proposals were substantial. Chief among
them was the assertion that voters should have an opportunity to express themselves on the amendment by choosing state legislators
with known positions on the subject, rather than leaving the decision
to legislators who had been elected previously for reasons unrelated
to those involved in the amendment.

On the constitutionality and rationality of the proposals, one
historian sums up the arguments as follows:

First, that by necessary implication Congress had the
power to make such regulations; secondly, that it is wise

and expedient to adopt some general rule by which there
shall be equal, fair, uniform, and timely action in the
several states; thirdly, that the plan proposed would give
all the advantages of a convention system without its
disadvantages of inconvenience and expense, for it would
give the people of every state a full and complete opportunity of passing upon the amendment; fourthly, that this
plan, by designating the legislature which shall act upon
the amendment, removes all possibility of question as to
what particular legislature or legislatures are to act upon
it, or as to the length of the time the amendment is open
for ratification. The difficulty of having amendments ratified and then having the ratification rescinded, or having
an amendment rejected and afterwards ratified by the legislature of the same state, both of which events had
occurred in the case of the recent [thirteenth and four-
teenth] amendments in several of the states, would be
avoided. [15]

Opponents of the motion pressed these arguments: there was no
precedent for such regulations; it would be unconstitutional to select
some future legislature to pass upon an amendment when Article V
obviously refers to legislatures in existence at the time an amendment
is submitted to the states; Congress has no right to withhold the ratification power from an existing legislature on the assumption that a
future body will act on the amendment; the record of 14 previous
amendments shows that a majority of the legislatures involved in the
ratification process had been chosen before the admendments were
submitted to them. Like the previous attempt to circumscribe the
ratification process, this one failed by a vote of 13 senators in favor,
43 opposed. [16]
    In more recent times an unusual opportunity to test the practica-
bility of ratification regulations arose when, for the first time, Congress directed that state conventions be called to consider ratification
of the amendment to repeal prohibition. In the course of discussion,
the question of federal funding of the cost of electing convention delegates led to a wholesale denunciation of federal controls of any sort.
Republican Senator John J. Blaine of Wisconsin was joined by Democratic Representative Emanuel Celler of New York in declaring that
Congress had no right to impose its will on the states in procedural
matters. Celler acknowledged that, left to their own devices, states
might come up with 48 different kinds of machinery, but he felt this
could not be helped. [17] Thus the states were given no instructions or
guidelines and, as Everett S. Brown's detailed study documents, the
procedures they devised were nearly as diverse as Celler had

anticipated. More disturbing than lack of uniformity was the casual approach to ratification taken by some states, a number of them treating the matter quite perfunctorily; Arkansas even failed to retain an official record of the action its convention took to approve the amendment. [18]

Because Congress has not attempted to go beyond the specific terms of Article V in directing the states as to procedures to be used in initiating or ratifying amendments, the Supreme Court has not answered any of the critical questions raised by such proposals. The debate of this subject continues, however, and the character of the arguments, and the court positions they presuppose, will be discussed in later chapters.

Q: What limits may be applied to the subject matter of amendments?

A: If, as the Supreme Court has said, the only limits placed upon Congress are those stipulated in Article V, then all subjects are fair game except the requirement of two-thirds approval by both houses of Congress and the prohibition against depriving any state of equal representation in the Senate. Yet, theoretically, even these limits may be removed by amendment of Article V. Because they were clearly intended by the framers to remain untouchable for all time, these two restrictions have been declared to have a quality of sanctity superior to the rest of the Constitution. But radical changes, some of them inconceivable to the men who drafted the Constitution, have been made in the original provisions. When suffrage was extended to former slaves by the Fifteenth Amendment and to women by the Nineteenth Amendment, and when by the Twenty-fourth Amendment states were forbidden to disenfranchise voters in federal elections for non-payment of taxes, the constitutional system of representation was altered very radically from the design of 1787. When prohibition was challenged on the very logical ground that the subject matter should be dealt with by ordinary legislation and not by an amendment unrelated to the country's basic law, the courts refused to adopt this restrictive interpretation. The door to unlimited subject matter was opened even wider by the Supreme Court's statement in a loyalty-oath case that "while the procedure for amending [the Constitution] is restricted, there is no restraint on the kind of amendment that may be offered."[19] When the Supreme Court rejected the claim that Congress has no power to deny states the right to decide who may vote, the change thus cemented into the constitutional foundation was as revolutionary, in terms of its original design, as a modification of Article V voting formulas would be.[20]

Clearly, only tradition provides protection against changes in those segments of Article V that both the framers and, subsequently, the courts have declared sacrosanct. The extraordinary strength of that tradition is seen in its ability to stand against the logic that says no one part of the basic law is more basic than another. Nevertheless, some of the current nervousness over the prospect of a new constitutional convention is undoubtedly attributable to an underlying suspicion that such a gathering might prove a serious threat to concepts that have long been taken for granted.

Other objections voiced frequently in recent years are aimed at attempts to embody in the Constitution what some believe as the goals of particular interest groups. These groups are not satisfied to run the risk of having ordinary legislation overturned, and therefore seek to achieve for their proposals the protection of fundamental law.[21]

Q: Must congressional approval of a resolution to amend the Constitution be by two-thirds of the full membership of each house? Must such a resolution include a specific statement that two-thirds of both houses deem the amendment necessary?

A: These questions, like so many others relating to the amendment procedure, were raised by objectors to the Prohibition Amendment and indicate the variety of technicalities that can be raised at every stage of the process. On the first question, the Supreme Court took what had, by 1920, become its normal approach to Article V: the only restrictions placed upon congressional procedure are those spelled out in specific terms in that article. Historically, Congress had never used any procedure for voting on amendments other than to require approval by two-thirds of the members present. The court accepted this custom by declaring the requirement to be "a vote of two-thirds of the members present—assuming the presence of a quorum—and not a vote of two-thirds of the entire membership, present and absent."[22]

The court responded to the second point with a clear negative, saying: "The adoption by both houses of Congress, each by a two-thirds vote, of a joint resolution proposing an amendment to the Constitution sufficiently shows that the proposal was deemed necessary by all who voted for it." Should a similar challenge arise with respect to the action of a national convention, state legislature, or convention, the same reasoning would apply. This is as significant for the states as it is for Congress, as procedures for approving other than normal legislation vary from one state to another.

Q: At what stages and under what circumstances may the amendment process be challenged in the courts?

A: Theoretically, the courts are open at all times to all persons with legitimate grievances, but effective challenges to the amendment process have been severely restricted by Supreme Court decisions. Many potential protests are foreclosed by the court's position that the ratification procedure is a federal function not subject to any limitation sought to be imposed by the people or legislature of a state.[23] Although this judgment was directed to the process of ratification only, it can as logically be applied to the initiation stage as well.

When a private individual attempted to contest the right of the secretary of state to promulgate the women's suffrage amendment, the Supreme Court held that a citizen's right to require that government be administered lawfully and public money not wasted does not entitle that individual "to institute in the federal courts a suit to secure by indirection whether a statute, if passed, or a constitutional amendment about to be adopted, will be valid."[24] An attempt to insist that the prohibition amendment be submitted to state conventions specially chosen by the people, on the ground that this amendment would confer upon the federal government new powers over individuals, was turned aside by the court's decision that the choice of method of ratification rests solely in the discretion of Congress.[25]

On questions that appear to involve political rather than legal judgments, the court has denied its own jurisdiction, insisting that such questions are for the elected representatives of the people to resolve. This position was expressed most forcefully in 1939 when, in a concurring opinion, Supreme Court Justices Black and Douglas stated: "We do not believe that State or Federal courts have any jurisdiction to interfere with the amending process."[26] On the other hand, the legal profession has expressed almost unanimous opposition to any plan that would arbitrarily exclude the courts from exercising jurisdiction over challenges to congressional rules for constitutional conventions.[27] Under the Black-Douglas interpretation, it is conceivable that a Congress strongly supportive of a particular amendment might ignore actions by states to reverse earlier resolutions of approval, while a Congress antagonistic to a pending amendment might accept such reversals as negating prior approvals. The latter position has not been taken for as long as Congress has been the initiator of new amendments. The likelihood of this path being taken increases, however, if the initial step is made by a constitutional convention acting independently of Congress, or if Congress enacts legislation regulating convention procedures and in the process makes it possible for states to rescind their earlier requests for a convention.[28]

Q: If two-thirds of the state legislatures request a convention, must Congress comply or may it substitute action by two-thirds of its own House and Senate?

A: This question has never faced the courts, but it arises because many persons in and out of Congress fear that once a constitutional convention has been called, there will be no control over what it will do. Further, a drive to stimulate two-thirds of the states to request a convention for a particular purpose might very well parallel an effort by members of Congress to secure passage of a resolution to amend the Constitution for the same purpose. On at least one occasion Congress was spurred to devise its own amendment to forestall action by the states to take up the matter in a convention. More recently, the drive for an amendment to require a balanced federal budget has produced a substantial number of resolutions for a congressionally initiated amendment and, simultaneously, a significant number of state petitions requesting a national convention. Many of the state petitions request Congress either to propose a balanced-budget amendment itself or to call a constitutional convention to do so.[29]

Except for matters that might be taken up in a constitutional convention, the overriding power of Congress in the control of amendment procedure is evident from the Supreme Court's repeated holding that Congress has sole discretion in matters of ratification procedure. It is but a step from this position to one that determines that even if a convention were requested by two-thirds of the states before Congress could reach agreement on its own resolution, Congress has the right to opt for initiation by the House and Senate rather than by a convention.

The prospect of a successful challenge to Congress's right to determine which amendment process is to be used, is conceivable only if Congress were to call a convention and, before that body could act, decide to offer a resolution of its own for ratification by the states.[30] Even here, the courts might have difficulty concluding that Congress had acted unconstitutionally, though questions as to motive and reasonableness of such an about-face might justifiably be raised. Should such a situation occur, it would reflect a level of domestic turmoil that could be resolved only by political, rather than legal, action. While the country does not appear to be approaching so critical a stage, the rapidly developing conflict between proponents of a constitutional convention and advocates of congressional initiative in the matter of a balanced-budget amendment suggests the probability of a showdown in the near future.

NOTES

1. Hawke v. Smith, 253 U.S. 227 (1920).
2. Rhode Island v. Palmer, 253 U.S. 386 (1920).
3. Some of the proposals for amending Article V are reported in Chapter 1.
4. Dillon v. Gloss, 256 U.S. 373 (1921).
5. Coleman v. Miller, 307 U.S. 433 (1939).
6. CR (daily), 6 October 1978, pp. S17318-19.
7. ERA Hearings. Although there was general agreement on the right of Congress to extend the ratification period, opinions varied as to the implications of such action with respect to the right of rescission. The latter subject is developed further in Chapter 6.
8. South Dakota's action was reported in the New York Times, 11 March 1979. Copies of state resolutions on file in the Office of the Federal Register show that, as of April 1979, that office had received notices of the withdrawal or rescission of earlier approvals by Idaho, Nebraska, and Tennessee. A withdrawal resolution passed by the Kentucky legislature had also been received, although it had been vetoed by the lieutenant governor.
9. Reprinted from Student Lawyer, © 1980, American Bar Association. This suit was brought by the Mountain States Legal Foundation on behalf of Arizona, a rejecting state, and Idaho, a rescinding state, as well as 38 members of the Arizona House of Representatives and 15 Idaho senators.
10. All quotations relating to this question are from the Supreme Court decision in Coleman v. Miller, 307 U.S. 433 (1939).
11. Leser v. Garnett, 258 U.S. 137 (1922), indicated that "duly authenticated" state actions referred to the U.S. secretary of state require that officer to certify the adoption of an amendment approved by three-fourths of the state legislatures. This responsibility was transferred to the general services administrator in 1950 by the Reorganization Act of 1949, U.S. Code, Title 5, Sec. 160.
12. Coleman v. Miller, 307 U.S. 433 (1939).
13. Ames, p. 288.
14. Ibid., p. 288.
15. Ibid., p. 289.
16. Ibid., p. 290.
17. Everett Somerville Brown, Ratification of the Twenty-first Amendment to the Constitution of the United States, pp. 4-5.
18. Ibid., p. 25.
19. Whitehill v. Elkins, 389 U.S. 57 (1967).
20. Fairchild v. Hughes, 258 U.S. 126 (1922).
21. This debate gets down to specifics when the question is whether or not a requirement for a balanced federal budget (or a

prohibition against abortion, school busing, and so forth) should be made part of the Constitution. For arguments relating to the balanced-budget amendment see infra, Chapter 4.

22. Rhode Island v. Palmer, 253 U.S. 386 (1920).

23. Leser v. Garnett, 258 U.S. 137 (1922).

24. Fairchild v. Hughes, 258 U.S. 130 (1922).

25. United States v. Sprague, 282 U.S. 716 (1931).

26. Chandler v. Wise, 307 U.S. 474 (1939).

27. See the concluding question raised by the American Bar Association regarding the Ervin bill, infra, Chapter 6.

28. For serious attempts to enact such legislation, see infra, Chapter 6.

29. For further detail on this point see Chapter 6.

30. In a somewhat different context (in which a convention may be called by referendum as well as by legislative act), Hawaii's constitution anticipates the possibility of conflicting amendments and stipulates that if both "are submitted to the electorate at the same election and both are approved, then the revision or amendment proposed by the convention shall prevail." Constitutions of the United States, vol. 2, p. 77.

# 4

## THE PROBLEM FOR THE 1980s

At the close of the 1787 convention, the constitutional changes most ardently sought were those that would guarantee against curtailment of personal rights and freedoms by the newly established central government. Widespread demand led to the quick adoption of the first ten amendments to the Constitution. Until shortly after the Civil War, protection of the individual against state as well as federal authority continued to be the subject of the most dramatic changes in the Constitution. Thus the Thirteenth, Fourteenth, and Fifteenth Amendments eliminated slavery and attempted, however inadequately, to protect the civil and political rights of former slaves, particularly against infringement by state agencies.

In the twentieth century, the majority of approved amendments have dealt with expansion of suffrage and the effectiveness of government operations. Five of the eleven amendments passed since 1900 have extended the voting privilege to increasing numbers of the population, and three are concerned with presidential succession and terms of office for the chief executive and legislators. The remaining three illustrate two varieties of dissatisfaction that appear to indicate the most powerful sources of conflict in the years to come: moral outrage and discontent with fiscal policy.[1] Prohibition was essentially a moral issue, as are the more recent problems of abortion, school busing, and prayer in public schools, all of which have been the subject of numerous proposals for constitutional amendments.[2] Coming in the wake of the more extended, and more nearly successful, campaigns for amendments to guarantee equal rights for women and to mandate a balanced federal budget, these moral crusades add to the growing feeling among substantial numbers of people that Congress has not been responsive to the real needs of the country.

The extent of overall public support for any one campaign cannot be determined with any degree of accuracy because the polling organizations, in recording opinions on particular issues, rarely probe specifically for attitudes toward amending the Constitution. An examination of Public Opinion Quarterly for the four years prior to July 1980, for example, reveals that although studies were made of attitudes toward government fiscal policies and abortion, none of the nationwide polls dealt with the desirability of amending the Constitution as a means of resolving these problems. The one canvass that did ask for opinions on an amendment to prohibit abortion was conducted in Ohio only.[3] However, the explosive potential of these campaigns can readily be demonstrated by a brief review of the trend each has taken in recent years.

## ANTIBUSING PROPOSALS

Amendments to prohibit the busing of public school students for purposes of desegregation began filtering into Congress even before the Supreme Court decided that busing was one of several acceptable methods of desegregating school systems. Louisiana and Mississippi petitioned for a constitutional convention to prohibit busing in 1970, while the subject was still in litigation. The decision reached by the court in 1971 came after years of struggle by civil rights groups to force school districts to desegregate in accordance with the findings and instructions of the Supreme Court in the Brown v. Board of Education cases.[4] When 16 years later the court scored the "dilatory tactics of many school authorities," and indicated approval of busing as one means of achieving integration,[5] the decision aroused a storm of protest from the many supporters of the "dilatory tactics." Reactions ranged from that of Senator Henry M. Jackson of Washington, who proposed a constitutional amendment that would prohibit mandatory busing while mandating equal education for all, to one introduced by Senators James B. Allen of Alabama and Sam Ervin of North Carolina, that would forbid assignment of students to schools based on "race, creed, color or economic class."[6] Periodically, state legislatures petitioned for a convention to incorporate a ban on busing into the Constitution.[7] The number of petitions never approached the 34 needed to mandate the calling of a convention under Article V. However, the matter quickly grew from a state-by-state protest to an issue recognized by the national political parties. The Democratic platform of 1972 asserted its support of desegregation and approved the "transportation of students" as one means of achieving that goal. The Republican platform of the same year was "irrevocably opposed to busing for racial balance," and pointed with pride to President Nixon's proposed Student Transportation Moratorium Act, which would "halt immediately all further court-ordered busing and give Congress time to devise permanent new arrangements for assuring desegregated, quality education. "[8] Four years later the Democratic platform again included racial desegregation as one of its goals, but with this cautious reference to busing: "Mandatory transportation of students beyond their neighborhoods for the purpose of desegregation remains a judicial tool of the last resort. " The 1976 Republican platform repeated its opposition to "forced busing" and went on to say: "If Congress continues to fail to act, we would favor consideration of an amendment to the Constitution forbidding the assignment of children to schools on the basis of race. "[9]

The drive for a constitutional amendment came to at least a temporary halt in 1979, when for the first time an antibusing amendment was brought to the floor of the House of Representatives. Forced out of committee by a rarely used discharge petition signed by a majority of the House membership, the motion not only failed to secure the two-thirds vote necessary to pass, but also fell several votes short of a majority. [10] Newspaper conjecture that this defeat might kill the movement for all time ignored the strength and persistence of busing opponents. That determination was evident in the increasingly strident tone taken by the Republican presidential platform in 1980. This platform condemned the busing concept and asserted that where the practice exists, "we must halt forced busing. "[11] The Democratic platform repeated, verbatim, the party's 1976 statement that characterized busing as "a judicial tool of the last resort. "[12]

## PRAYER IN PUBLIC SCHOOLS

Even as Congress was in the process of closing the door to a school busing amendment, a drive for the return of prayer to the schoolroom was gathering momentum. Like the busing problem, the debate over public prayer had been triggered some years earlier by a decision of the Supreme Court. In response to a protest against required prayers, the court ruled in 1962 that "by using its public school system to encourage recitation of the Regents' prayer, the State of New York had adopted a practice wholly inconsistent with the Establishment Clause" of the First Amendment. [13] It confirmed this ruling the following year when it struck down a Pennsylvania statute that required daily reading of verses from the Bible. [14]

Periodically over the years that followed, bills aimed at overturning these decisions were introduced in Congress. To avoid the appearance of official sanction of prayers of any particular religion or sect, the bills were most often phrased to permit "voluntary prayer." Failure to gain approval of such legislation led to the adoption of other techniques, including the submission of constitutional amendments. These came sporadically from state legislatures and in periodic waves from federal lawmakers.[15] However, state petitions did not approach the number that would require Congress to take action, and the more numerous resolutions by members of the Congress all died in committee.

As presidential election year 1980 opened, a new surge of activity in the House of Representatives brought amendment proposals from Tim Lee Carter of Kentucky, Jamie L. Whitten of Mississippi, and Lamar Gudger of North Carolina. During the same period, the state of Washington petitioned Congress to draw up an amendment to approve prayer in the public schools.[16]

Another old and well-established tactic was called upon when public prayer provisions were attached to bills on other subjects that were more likely to receive congressional approval. One of the most controversial examples of the use of this maneuver was the "Helms amendment," moved by Senator Jesse Helms of North Carolina, which proposed to amend not the Constitution, but a bill dealing with the federal courts. Viewed by many as setting a dangerous precedent in attempting to legislate constitutional change, the amendment's objective was to remove from the jurisdiction of the federal courts consideration of any issue involving voluntary school prayer. The bill was passed by the Senate in 1979 and referred to the House of Representatives, where the battle for passage was taken up by Philip M. Crane of Illinois.[17] Temporarily stopped by a reluctant Judiciary Committee, Crane circulated a discharge petition that, with 218 signatures (a majority of the House membership), would force the measure to the floor of the House for a vote. Though he had not secured the required number of signatures when Congress adjourned for the 1980 presidential nominating conventions, Crane succeeded in forcing the House Judiciary Committee to schedule hearings on the Helms amendment. This is where the matter stood when Congress recessed in July 1980.

If any mention of the subject of school prayer arose in Democratic conferences on the party platform, it was not significant enough to warrant time or space in the media. On the Republican side, however, the question was very much in the news. Reportedly at the insistence of Senator Helms, the Republican platform committee approved the following statement:

We support Republican initiatives in the Congress to restore the right of individuals to participate in voluntary, non-denominational prayer in schools and other public facilities.[18]

Before the end of July, the renewal of Representative Crane's campaign made news in two successive issues (July 30 and 31) of the Washington Post. Even though at this stage the movement was not toward a constitutional convention, the rising pitch of debate gave clear warning that the subject was one that would continue to stimulate the demand for constitutional change. This change is desired by people who see immorality and degradation of religion and the American family as threats to what they consider the most important elements in American life, threats they feel are being fostered by the courts' "perverted" view of the Constitution.[19]

## THE ABORTION CONTROVERSY

The intensity of feeling exhibited by advocates of a school prayer amendment is more than matched by that of proponents of an anti-abortion amendment. For many years state laws made abortion illegal in almost every situation except when the mother's life was in danger. Challenges to these laws were frequent during the 1960s, and by 1972 the first cases reached the Supreme Court. When the case of Roe v. Wade was decided early in 1973, the impact on state abortion laws and controls was traumatic. Contrary to the view expressed in most state statutes, the Supreme Court found that the right of privacy, although not referred to explicitly in the Constitution, is implicit in the Fourteenth Amendment and "is broad enough to encompass a woman's decision whether or not to terminate her pregnancy."[20] Acknowledging that such a decision is not without limits, the court summarized its position as follows:

> 1. A state criminal abortion statute of the current Texas type, that excepts from criminality only a life-saving procedure on behalf of the mother, without regard to pregnancy state and without recognition of the other interests involved, is violative of the Due Process Clause of the Fourteenth Amendment.
> (a) For the stage prior to approximately the end of the first trimester, the abortion decision and its effectuation must be left to the medical judgment of the pregnant woman's attending physician.
> (b) For the stage subsequent to approximately the end of the first trimester, the State, in promoting its interest in the health of the mother, may, if it chooses,

regulate the abortion procedure in ways that are reasonably related to maternal health.

(c) For the stage subsequent to viability, the State in promoting its interest in the potentiality of human life may, if it chooses, regulate, and even proscribe, abortion except where it is necessary in appropriate medical judgment, for the preservation of the life and health of the mother [the court's emphasis].[21]

Reactions to this curb upon state autonomy were immediate, both for and against the decision. The care with which anti-abortion forces had monitored the progress of the legal proceedings taken to the Supreme Court is suggested by the action of the Indiana legislature. Twenty-four hours before the court's decision was made public, the Indiana legislature requested Congress to call a constitutional convention to uphold the states' position on abortion.[22] Members of Congress also entered the fray, some during the months preceding the court's hearing of the Roe case. In mid-1972, Representative Bella Abzug of New York, a leading advocate of the view that the prospective mother should make the decision as to an abortion, bolstered her arguments with exhibits and case studies that, on a single occasion, ran to 137 closely printed pages in the Congressional Record. Months later, after the court had made its opinion known, Senator James L. Buckley, also from New York, offered the other side of the case with remarks, exhibits, and contributions from other senators covering 27 pages.[23] Many legislators introduced amendments proposing to overturn the court's decision. Identical texts were submitted in the Senate by Jesse Helms of North Carolina, and in the House of Representatives by Lawrence J. Hogan of Maryland. All told, 32 anti-abortion amendments were introduced during 1973, the year of the Roe v. Wade decision, most of them originating in the House of Representatives.[24] This contrasts with the single amendment that had been submitted the year before.

Like the efforts to overturn Supreme Court decisions regarding busing and school prayer, those directed at the abortion decision failed for lack of a consensus on both the objective and the proper method of achieving it. Many of the legislators who favored strict control of abortion were unwilling to see this made the subject of a constitutional amendment. But neither the interest nor the pressure ceased. As time went on, the anti-abortion movement made a substantial impact on election campaigns. The major party platforms of 1972 avoided any reference to abortion, though the Democratic statement on family planning said it would "permit individuals freely to determine the number and spacing of their children." George C. Wallace's American Party, however, set the direction that later would be taken by the Republican Party when the former Democratic governor of Alabama announced his party's opposition to "all attempts to liberalize any anti-abortion laws. "[25] By 1976 the subject was unavoidable, and the two major parties took opposing sides on the question of a constitutional amendment. The Republican platform promised to "support the efforts of those who seek enactment of a constitutional amendment to restore protection of the right to life for unborn children," while the Democrats felt "it is undesirable to attempt to amend the U. S. Constitution to overturn Supreme Court decisions in this area." Both, however, were careful to acknowledge the existence of more than one point of view on abortion.[26]

Over the next four years there was no evidence of any cooling on this issue, or of a willingness to compromise, either in Congress or among organizations lobbying the two sides of the question. On the contrary, by 1980 the abortion issue had assumed an importance greater than at any time since the period immediately after the Supreme Court decision in Roe v. Wade. Members of the Senate and House of Representatives decried the growth of abortion to a "big business" that kills "literally millions" of Americans every year in "abortion mills." The "March for Life," organized by anti-abortionists in 1974 as a means of demonstrating to the legislators on Capitol Hill the strength of the sentiment for overturning the court's action, brought an estimated 100,000 marchers to Washington on the seventh anniversary of the Roe v. Wade decision. The efforts and objectives of this group were extolled by sympathizers in Congress, who combined their praise with pleas for renewed attention to the need for legislation or a constitutional amendment to remedy the damage inflicted on American society by the Supreme Court.[27] In addition to speeches on the floor of the House and Senate, some members used the growing practice of "revising and extending their remarks" to insert into the Congressional Record speeches and articles not actually presented on the floor, but which could nevertheless be mailed to constituents as evidence of their support.

During the early months of 1980, a new flow of petitions came to Congress from state legislatures. Most of these, in requesting Congress either to propose or call a convention to propose a right-to-life amendment to the Constitution, cited the Supreme Court's decision as the cause of the problem. The South Dakota petition went so far as to express the state legislature's "extreme disappointment, frustration and disagreement" with the court's action, in a manner more characteristic of memorials from private organizations. Of the seven petitions received from January to early May 1980, four demanded that Congress call a convention, stating flatly that this method was requested because "the Congress of the United States has not to date proposed . . . a right-to-life amendment."[28]

By the summer of 1980, the campaign for an anti-abortion amendment had been adopted officially by the Republican Party, which included the following statement in a section of its presidential platform devoted specifically to this subject:

> There can be no doubt that the question of abortion, despite the complex nature of its various issues, is ultimately concerned with equality of rights under the law. While we recognize differing views on this question among Americans in general—and in our own Party—we affirm our support of a constitutional amendment to restore protection of the right to life for unborn children. We also support the congressional efforts to restrict the use of taxpayers' dollars for abortion.
>
> We protest the Supreme Court's intrusion into the family structure through its denial of the parents' obligation and right to guide their minor children.[29]

The Democratic platform dealt with this subject first under the heading, "Reproductive Rights," which opened with the following paragraphs:

> We fully recognize the religious and ethical concerns which many Americans have about abortion. We also recognize the belief of many Americans that a woman has a right to choose whether and when to have a child.
>
> The Democratic Party supports the 1973 Supreme Court decision on abortion rights as the law of the land and opposes any constitutional amendment to restrict or overturn that decision.

A later reference to the same subject, but aimed at efforts to control abortion by statute rather than by constitutional amendment, was contained in a statement on privacy that read:

> The Democratic Party recognizes reproductive freedom as a fundamental human right. We therefore oppose government interference in the reproductive decisions of Americans, especially those government programs or legislative restrictions that deny poor Americans their right to privacy by funding or advocating one or a limited number of reproductive choices only.[30]

The only significant challenger to the two major-party candidates for the presidency, John B. Anderson, made abortion a front-line issue in his campaign. Writing on the stationery of the National Abortion Rights League, Anderson circulated to voters a letter condemning the attempt to "defeat those who have defended a woman's right to choose." Confirming what his opponents on this issue had made no effort to hide, he called attention to the "hit list" of U.S. senators and representatives that anti-abortionists had compiled as targets for defeat in the 1980 congressional elections. He accused this "reactionary coalition of right wing groups" of attempting to destroy the political careers of "some of the nation's most progressive leaders," and of being indirectly responsible for "the burning and vandalism of abortion clinics . . . harassment of patients . . . political intimidation . . . and the growing threat of a Constitutional Convention." He described their "loud and clear" message to Congress in these terms:

> "Vote for every piece of anti-abortion legislation including a constitutional amendment to reverse the Supreme Court's decision on abortion. Better to go along with us than to suffer the political punishment we can deliver."[31]

A suggestion that some in Congress may have interpreted the message in the same way as Anderson came with the news that in August 1980 the House of Representatives passed, by a 228 to 170 vote, a rider to an appropriation bill that would forbid the funding of abortions—for any purpose including saving a life—under any health plan for federal employees.[32]

It was in this bitter atmosphere that the pro- and anti-abortion forces prepared for the fall 1980 elections.


## THE EQUAL RIGHTS AMENDMENT

None of the campaigns described above has come as close to its goal as the one dedicated to passage of an equal rights amendment. The progress made by ERA proponents has been the result of success in securing enough support in Congress for an amendment to be initiated there, with subsequent ratification by state legislatures. Thus ERA has followed the traditional path of amendment rather than the path of a national convention. This does not rule out a convention attempt if opponents of ERA succeed in defeating the proposal by means of one of the three methods they have adopted as countermeasures: winning a negative vote in each state legislature that considers the amendment, thus preventing approval by the three additional states needed (as of July 1980) to reach the 38 required for ratification; successfully challenging the legality of state approvals made subsequent to 22 March 1979, the original deadline for ratification set by Congress; or convincing the courts that states that have rescinded their earlier ratifications should not be counted as having ratified. A suit citing these alleged illegalities was filed in 1979 on behalf of two of the protesting states (Arizona and Idaho) to prevent the General Services Administrator from certifying the ratification of the Equal Rights Amendment.[33]

The increasingly frantic struggle of ERA proponents to obtain approval by 38 states before the extended deadline arrives reached a feverish pitch in 1979-80. Even religion, which has played a more overt role in the moral issues discussed above, became a factor in the legal battle over the time extension and the question of rescission. Federal Judge Marion Callister, before whom the Arizona-Idaho challenge was brought, was then regional representative of the Mormon Church. The case went to court as some female members of that church were protesting church policy on ERA and the right of women to assume positions of authority in the church hierarchy. ERA supporters charged that official Mormon policy was in "opposition to both the Equal Rights Amendment and the extension" of the deadline for ratification. Because of this, and because Judge Callister was "near the top of the church hierarchy," the Justice Department filed a motion asking him to disqualify himself. Judge Callister refused.[34]

The bitterness of the ERA contest was heightened in summer 1980 by the turnabout of the Republican Party at its presidential nominating convention. Abandoning its pro-ERA position of some 40 years, the convention approved a "women's rights" plank that included the following paragraph:

> Ratification of the Equal Rights Amendment is now in
> the hands of state legislatures, and the issues of the
> time extension and rescission are in the courts. The
> states have a constitutional right to accept or reject a
> constitutional amendment without federal interference
> or pressure. At the direction of the White House,
> federal departments launched pressure against states
> which refused to ratify ERA. Regardless of one's
> position on ERA, we demand that this practice cease.[35]

Notwithstanding the absence of a flat repudiation of ERA, this stand proved one of the few divisive elements coming out of the Republican convention. It led to such important defections among Republican women as former party cochairperson Mary Crisp, who became national chairperson of John B. Anderson's presidential

campaign.[36] Both Anderson and the Democratic Party confirmed
their support of ERA. The Democratic convention made a point of
highlighting the matter in an "Equal Rights Amendment" plank that
read, in part:

> The Democratic Party must insure that ERA at last
> becomes the 27th Amendment to the Constitution. We
> oppose efforts to rescind ERA in states which have
> already ratified the amendment, and we shall insist
> that past rescissions are invalid.
>    The Democratic Party shall withhold financial sup-
> port and technical campaign assistance from candi-
> dates who do not support the ERA. The Democratic
> Party further urges all national organizations to sup-
> port the boycott of the unratified states by not holding
> national meetings, conferences, or conventions in
> those states.

The latter paragraph caused understandable dismay among a number
of Democrats who had already taken a stand against the amendment.[37]

The history of ERA is unique in several respects. As opinion
polls have indicated, it has stimulated literally millions of people to
think about a subject that most recognize as a constitutional problem.
The drive for full equality has also aroused the interest of a significant portion of the population to a demand that is as old as the
women's suffrage movement, which came into its own three-quarters
of a century earlier. Even assuming that a large segment of the
population is indifferent or undecided as to the outcome of the contest, the disposition of the ERA proposal will, in fact, directly
affect the entire female population, which makes up more than 50
percent of the total, and indirectly, most of the male remainder.
Finally, to the student of constitutional history or law, the case
provides a fascinating collection of material for the study of all the
ramifications and implications of Article V of the United States
Constitution.


## PROPOSALS FOR A BALANCED-BUDGET AMENDMENT

As the decade of the 1980s opened, the most frenzied campaigns for constitutional amendment were undoubtedly those conducted
by pro-ERA and anti-abortion organizations. But the drive most
likely to bring the problem of a constitutional convention to a head
was, and will continue to be, the one for an amendment that would
mandate a balanced federal budget. The protest movement generated

by discontent in this area has become so widespread, and has enlisted so much support for a national assembly to amend the Constitution, that it provides an excellent base from which to consider the critical problem of a constitutional convention.

Concern with federal finance is hardly a new phenomenon in American politics. From the country's earliest days, the cost of government has been a source of lively discussion. Although the early history of constitutional development saw vigorous, often bitter, debate on questions relating to the powers that should be relinquished by the states to the central government, there was little argument over giving Congress fairly broad powers to raise and spend money "for the common defense and general welfare." Even the authority to borrow money was approved by the 1787 convention, though a proposal to permit the issuance of "bills of credit," which raised the spectre of paper money of the sort that had become almost worthless during the Revolution, was rejected by that body. For if the phrase "not worth a continental" was appropriately descriptive of the value of the paper dollar issued by the confederation during the Revolutionary War, it was even more expressive of the assorted paper currencies printed by the states. One of the ironies of the situation reached two hundred years later is that the federal government, which was established in part to remedy the disastrous economic effects of fiscal irresponsibility at the state level, itself faces charges of fiscal irresponsibility that may force Congress to call a convention aimed at curtailing the very authority that originally was intended to save the nation from financial disaster.

For the first century and a half of constitutional government, the nation as a whole assumed that federal budgets would be designed to produce income sufficient to cover anticipated expenditures, and that borrowing would be limited to special or emergency situations. Deficits were not uncommon during wartime, but were otherwise regarded as unnecessary. Indeed, by 1833 surpluses had been accumulated with sufficient regularity to lead the Georgia legislature to suggest a convention to amend the federal Constitution in such a way as to "prescribe what distribution shall be made of the surplus revenue."[38] By the latter part of the nineteenth century, however, what one historian characterized as "the increasing extravagance of the appropriation bills" enacted by Congress began a trend in the opposite direction. The frequent use of riders attached to appropriation measures, often at the last minute and without due consideration, prompted President Ulysses S. Grant to recommend in 1873 an amendment that would authorize the chief executive to exercise an item veto.[39] Many states have given their governors this authority, both before and after Grant proposed it for the president, but Congress would have none of it.

Within the executive branch, the first time the Secretary of the Treasury saw fit to include revenue estimates in his annual report was in 1907; only in 1909 did Congress decide to require executive budget proposals to consider expenditures in the light of receipts. [40] Denunciations of extravagance and waste had long been standard campaign rhetoric, but in 1916 both Democratic and Republican Party platforms promised a new "budget system. "[41] Significant progress in this direction was made in 1921 when the Budget and Accounting Act was passed, and expenditures and revenues were incorporated into the official federal budget for the first time. Fifteen years later, the first two proposals to require a balanced federal budget were introduced into Congress: one a draft statute offered by Representative W. D. McFarlane of Texas, the other a suggested amendment to the Constitution by Representative Harold Knutson of Minnesota. [42]

The general assumption that income and expenditures would be kept in rough balance from year to year did not give way until the Great Depression of the 1930s, when extreme financial crisis and an unemployment rate of almost 25 percent indicated the need for unusual measures. Until that time, no president or congress had adopted deficit spending as a deliberate policy to relieve the pressures of poverty or to stimulate economic activity. Republican administrations before and after the depression have consistently rejected such an approach to the solution of economic problems, even in periods of high unemployment and/or slumping business activity. But regardless of the party in power, the unrelenting pressure of mounting expenditures for military and social programs in the decades following World War II was reflected in deficit budgeting that, by the country's bicentennial year, had become almost a way of life for the federal government, and for many states and municipalities as well. At the federal level, the national debt had grown from $16 billion or $131 per person in 1930, to the awesome level of $620 billion or $2,883 per person in 1976. President Carter's original goal of a balanced budget by 1980—the year in which he expected to run for reelection—was coupled with the grim forecast of a national debt of $847 billion, almost $4,000 per person, before leveling off could be achieved.

Annual assurances that "temporary" deficits were necessary to resolve serious economic conditions did not stem the growing conviction that continued government spending in excess of income was a primary cause of the inflation that, by 1980, had eroded public purchasing power to a serious degree. [43] Nor could these assurances still complaints that reliance on statutory controls as a means of achieving a balanced budget had been tried and found wanting. Proponents of a constitutional amendment pointed to continued deficits after passage of the Congressional Budget Act of 1974, and to their unsuccessful last-minute attempt in April 1979 to amend the debt-ceiling bill with a balanced-budget provision. This latter effort was defeated after House Ways and Means Committee Chairman Al Ullman told the House that debate on this question should be put over until the budget was discussed lest "for the first time in the history of the United States of America, it will default on its obligations unless the bill . . . to increase the public debt limit is passed by the House today and is sent to the President for his signature."[44]

The year 1980 brought campaign demands for immediate tax cuts from the Republicans and promises of cuts "next year" from the Democrats. Long before election day, the prospect of a balanced budget receded further into the future as, in two successive issues of the Washington Post (August 21 and 22), tax cuts recommended by the Senate Finance Committee were reported as climbing from $33 billion one day to $39 billion a day later. On October 30, less than a week before election day, the New York Times reported the federal deficit for fiscal year 1980 as $59 billion, the second highest deficit on record.

The very cost of debt service gave added impetus to the drive for a constitutional amendment.[45] In 1976, the interest on the public debt of the federal government amounted to nearly 27 percent of the total amount collected annually in individual income taxes. This ratio was expected to remain unchanged even as tax collections increased.[46]

Added to the burden resulting from heavy federal spending were mounting state, county, and municipal taxes and expenditures. Cities like Cleveland, Newark, and New York reached a point at which they were forced to make serious cuts in spending and in services to avoid default on their obligations. Many states felt the pinch as well, but the first successful statewide revolt against public financial policy occurred in a jurisdiction that had enjoyed a surplus, rather than a deficit, for five consecutive years. Despite this condition of affluence (perhaps partly because of it), the citizens of California in 1978 voted approval of the now-famous Proposition 13. Passed over the combined opposition of the governor, legislative leaders, city mayors, and most of the business and labor community, the measure forced an immediate reduction of property taxes by 57 percent, and established serious barriers to further increases.[47]

The action of California voters in June 1978 set the pattern for similar steps in 13 other states in the following November elections. In all of these states, from North Dakota to Alabama and Massachusetts to Hawaii, voters approved initiatives to limit government spending or taxes or both. So powerful was this movement that it stimulated the introduction of a wide range of initiatives relating to busing, gambling, equal rights for women and homosexuals, nuclear

power, and many other controversial subjects.[48] However, relatively few of the nonfiscal items were approved.

Revolt at the state level brought to the fore a drive for federal
action that had started, with less fanfare, not long after World War
II. Income taxes were the first target. Except for a brief period
during World War I, maximum income tax rates never exceeded 25
percent from passage of the Sixteenth Amendment in 1913 through
1931. However, during the depression of the 1930s they soared to
79 percent, then to 94 percent during World War II, falling back
only as far as 82 percent in the immediate postwar period.[49] Although the tax laws contained many loopholes for people in high-
income brackets, by 1950 conservative leaders in Congress were
attempting to reduce the tax ceiling sharply, either by legislation or
constitutional amendment.[50]

Over the next decade the focus of attack moved from tax ceilings to enforcement of a balanced budget. Constitutional amendments
were proposed by Senators Harry Flood Byrd of Virginia and Henry
Styles Bridges of New Hampshire to require "that the President submit a balanced budget, and that Congress could not adjourn without
enacting a balanced budget."[51] As deficit spending continued and
the public debt mounted to unprecedented heights, the attack intensi-
fied, gaining widespread public support as the cost of living began to
spiral. By the mid-1970s Congress was receiving petitions from
state legislatures demanding one of two actions: congressional approval and submission to the states of a constitutional amendment
mandating a balanced federal budget, or a congressional resolution
calling for a constitutional convention to deal with this problem. Although most states offered Congress the option of initiating the
amendment by its own resolution, an "or else" condition in the form
of a request for a national convention was attached to 10 of the first
22 petitions submitted. These were supported by 11 others that
called for a convention without giving Congress the option of devising
its own amendment. Of the 22 petitioning states, only Texas asked
for congressional action without any reference to a convention.[52]

The demand for a convention to limit government spending by
constitutional amendment is a reminder of the long-standing suspicion
many voters have had about the reluctance of federal legislators to
curtail their own powers or prerogatives. This suspicion is not
allayed by Congress's record of burying the many amendment
proposals submitted by its own members, allowing them to die in
committee, most often without even a hearing. In spring 1979,
Representative E. Thomas Coleman of Missouri warned of the
"grave mistake" Congress was making in ignoring both its own
members' balanced-budget proposals and petitions from state legis-

latures requesting a constitutional convention to design such an
amendment. [53] In the Senate, Dennis DeConcini of Arizona sounded
a similar warning and attempted to force consideration of his amendment by offering it as a floor amendment to a resolution dealing with
an entirely different matter. [54]

A major source of support in the attack on federal spending
comes from a segment of the public that is opposed to "big government" as such, to massive public expenditures for welfare and
other benefit programs aimed at individual (rather than corporate)
members of society, and to federal controls in areas such as education that have long been considered matters of local jurisdiction.
Population groups holding grievances against these characteristics
of federal operations provide the greatest driving force behind the
demand for a balanced-budget amendment—by convention if necessary.

Opposition to change by constitutional convention centers
principally about two aspects of the problem. The first one deals
with the substantive merits of a balanced budget, and raises questions
as to the advisability of anchoring in the Constitution a budget principle that might prove disastrously inflexible not only in crisis situations, but also as an impediment to action needed to avert crises or
wild swings in the economy. [55]

The second aspect is the quaking fear felt by many people, in
government and out, that turning the question of a constitutional
amendment over to a national convention would be courting disaster.
In this, political liberals, whose opposition to a balanced-budget
amendment is based largely on the restrictions it would impose on
government, are joined by conservatives who desire these restrictions but distrust the convention system as a means of achieving
them. Representatives of all political persuasions are uneasy about
the possible outcome of a convention having no precedent to guide it
in matters of membership selection, organization, and procedure.
Without even the dubious assurance of knowing how delegates would
be chosen, the fear is that such a gathering might include some who
would not be content with only devising a balanced-budget amendment,
but would take advantage of the opportunity to release other pent-up
frustrations in a wholesale attack on more basic elements of the
Constitution. On this score, as conservative a critic of government
spending as Howard Jarvis, co-author of California's Proposition
13, has been quoted as condemning a balanced-budget convention as
a move that "would put the Constitution back on the drawing board,
where every radical crackpot or special-interest group would have
the chance to write the supreme law of the land."[56] A similar view
was expressed by conservative Senator John C. Stennis of Mississippi
who, while arguing in favor of a balanced-budget amendment,
strongly opposed the use of a convention to initiate such a change.

"I am alarmed and frightened by the very prospect," he told the Senate Subcommittee on the Constitution. Challenging the view that Congress has the power to limit the scope of a convention, Stennis summed up the major concerns of convention opponents as follows:

> Even assuming, as an abstract legal question, that
> Congress has this power, the question is: How is it
> to be enforced: What is there to insure that the con-
> vention would not become a "runaway" assembly which
> would try to rewrite our basic law in numerous particu-
> lars? There are too many unanswered and unanswerable
> legal questions and problems involved to make the con-
> vention procedure worthy of the risk involved. [57]

Notwithstanding the many protests against action by a convention, the prospect of such a development becomes more real as
state resolutions demanding this procedure—at least as an alternative
if Congress refuses to act—continue to mount. By 1980, 30 balanced-
budget petitions had been received, only four short of the number
needed to force Congress to call a convention. [58]

Many members of Congress have submitted or supported joint
resolutions aimed at obtaining a balanced-budget amendment by the
normal route of congressional initiation followed by ratification by
state legislatures. [59] But notwithstanding the substantial number of
such proposals, none has been cleared by the appropriate Senate or
House committee for general debate by all members of the national
legislature. Constant pressure led the chairman of the Senate
Judiciary Committee to promise hearings on proposals introduced in
1979, and hearings were held to consider 20 separate resolutions.
The hearings concluded November 1 of that year. [60] After the subcommittee had voted 5 to 2 to pass the measure on to the full
Judiciary Committee, continued pressure eventually forced the
committee to vote on whether or not to send a particular amendment
to the floor of the Senate for consideration by the entire body. This
motion was defeated by the narrowest of margins, 9 to 8. [61] In April
1980, pro-amendment Senator Orin G. Hatch of Utah issued the following warning to the Senate:

> Although we were unsuccessful on this occasion, I re-
> mind my colleagues who oppose this or any other con-
> stitutional amendment on the balanced budget that they
> had better not breathe a sigh of relief quite yet. The
> hard fact remains that there are 30 sovereign States
> that have applied to this body for a constitutional con-
> vention on the subject of a balanced budget amendment.

> Upon the receipt of valid applications by two-thirds of
> the States, 34, Congress under Article V of the Consti-
> tution is "obliged" to call such a convention. [62]

The history of proposals for balanced-budget, equal rights,
anti-abortion, and other amendments with wide popular support
clearly demonstrates that it is not sufficient to decry the notion of
a convention on the ground that it would involve too many unknowns.
Even though this fear may well drive Congress to come up with some
kind of compromise amendment to avert a convention call, the need
to face up to the prospect of a convention still exists. If it does not
come by way of a drive for budgetary controls, it will be forced on
some other issue, with abortion as the next most likely candidate.
As indicated in the following chapters, a number of senators and
representatives have agreed that it would be better to meet the growing likelihood of such a development by anticipating particular problems and devising solutions to them, than to continue putting off a
confrontation and eventually be caught unprepared.

## NOTES

1. Amendment no. 16, authorizing income taxes, ratified
1913; no. 17, popular election of senators, 1913; no. 18, prohibition,
1919; no. 19, women's suffrage, 1920; no. 20, presidential term
and succession, 1933; no. 21, repeal of prohibition, 1933; no. 22,
two-term limit for presidency, 1951; no. 23, vote for District of
Columbia residents in presidential elections, 1961; no. 24, poll tax
invalid for federal elections, 1964; no. 25, presidential inability,
1967; no. 26, voting age 18, 1971.
2. A summary of state applications to Congress for a constitutional convention from January 1974 to September 1977 is
printed in CR (daily), 2 November 1977, pp. S18498-99. Of the
32 petitions on this list, 11 request a balanced-budget convention,
10 call for one on abortion, and 3 on busing. For the prior
decade (1963-73), the distribution of convention requests was:
balanced budget, two; abortion, one; busing, six; school prayer,
seven. See Library of Congress, Congressional Research Service,
"State Applications to Congress Calling for Conventions to Propose
Constitutional Amendments (January, 1963 to April 3, 1973)."
3. For reports on the taxing-spending problem, see Public
Opinion Quarterly, Spring 1979, pp. 126-35. Attitudes toward
abortion are reviewed in Winter 1977-78, pp. 553-64 and Summer
1979, pp. 181-89.
In 1972 Senator Richard Schweiker of Pennsylvania inserted

into the Congressional Record a report published by Citizens for Public Prayer, which listed a number of polls on prayer in public places. However, all but one were limited to single congressional districts, cities, or readers of particular periodicals. The single exception was identified as "a national poll conducted for the TV program, 'The Advocates,' by Opinion Research," and purported to show that 80 percent of those polled favored an amendment to permit prayer in public schools. The basis for the polling sample was not indicated. CR, vol. 118, pp. 13,412-15.

4. Commonly referred to as Brown I and Brown II. The first case, Brown v. Board of Education, 347 U.S. 483 (1954), resulted in racial segregation being declared unconstitutional; in the second stage of Brown v. Board of Education, 349 US. 294 (1955), the court considered "the manner in which relief is to be accorded," concluding that this must be accomplished in light of local circumstances, including "the school transportation system."

5. Swann v. Charlotte-Mecklenburg County Board of Education, 402 U.S. 1 (1971).

6. S.J. Res. 203 and 207, CR vol. 118 (1972), pp. 3740, 4777-78.

7. See note 2.

8. Donald Bruce Johnson, comp., National Party Platforms, vol. 2, pp. 804, 865-66.

9. Ibid., pp. 926-27, 974.

10. New York Times, 25 July 1979.

11. Republican National Committee, "Republican Platform," 14 July 1980, p. 15.

12. Democratic National Committee, "Democratic Platform," 1980, p. 8.

13. Engel v. Vitale, 370 U.S. 421, 424 (1962).

14. School District of Abington Township v. Schempp, 374 U.S. 203 (1963).

15. State petitions were received from North Dakota in 1963, Massachusetts in 1964, Maryland in 1966, Arizona in 1972, Mississippi and New Hampshire in 1973. Massachusetts submitted a second petition in 1967 to give specific approval to Bible reading. Congressional Research Service, "State Applications (January, 1963 to April 3, 1973)," and "State Applications Received from June 9, 1973 through March 24, 1976." In 1973, 7 amendments were proposed by members of the U.S. Senate and 34 by representatives in the House. The following year no amendments on prayer were introduced, but in 1975 a new wave appeared, 7 in the Senate and 52 in the House. CR, vol. 119, index, p. 327; vol. 121, index, p. 303.

16. CR (daily), pp. H295, H388, H2464, S2806.

17. The joint Crane-Helms statement of purpose and plan of attack was printed in CR (daily), 28 January 1980, p. E138.

18. "Republican Platform," 1980, p. 15.

19. See the "Declaration of Voluntary School Prayer" of the Association of National Religious Broadcasters, printed in CR (daily), 29 January 1980, p. S539, at the request of Senator Helms. This association represents principally evangelical groups, which are the strongest supporters of public prayer in general, and the Helms amendment in particular. As a Washington Post report of 30 July 1980 noted, representatives of other religious groups, including the National Council of Churches, Baptist Joint Committee on Public Affairs, and the Anti-Defamation League of B'nai B'rith, expressed some concern about the dangers of Helms's approach.

20. Roe v. Wade, 410 U.S. 113, 153 (1973).

21. Ibid., 164-65.

22. Congressional Research Service, "State Applications Received 1973-1976."

23. CR, vol. 118 (1972), pp. 15,327-64; vol. 119 (1973), pp. 17,538-65.

24. CR, vol. 119, S.J. Res. 119 and 130, H.J. Res. 261, pp. 17,569, 22,225; index, p. 327.

25. Johnson, National Party Platforms, vol. 2, pp. 796, 771.

26. Ibid., pp. 976, 926.

27. For a few of many examples, see CR (daily), 22 and 23 January 1980, when the March for Life assembled for its annual parade in Washington.

28. The petitions of West Virginia, Idaho, Massachusetts, South Dakota, Oklahoma, Tennessee, and Alabama, received in that order, are reproduced in full in CR (daily), 7 February 1980, p. S1247-48; 21 March, p. S2804; 28 March, p. S3250; 18 April, p. S3932; 24 April, p. S4202; 2 May, p. S4499; 9 May, p. S5095. The states that demanded a convention were Idaho, Oklahoma, Tennessee, and Alabama.

29. "Republican Platform," 1980, p. 13.

30. "Democratic Platform," 1980, pp. 5, 11-12.

31. From a form letter received by the author 14 August 1980.

32. Washington Post, 22 August 1980.

33. See note 9, Chapter 3.

34. CR (daily), 20 December 1979. This summary was given on the floor of the House of Representatives by Elizabeth Holtzman of New York, who went on to cite the church's excommunication of a Mormon woman supporter of ERA, and editorials in the New York Times and Boston Globe that raised serious questions of a conflict of interest between Judge Callister's high position in the Mormon Church

and his position as judge of an issue on which his church had taken an an official and unequivocal stand.

35. "Republican Platform," 1980, p. 10.

36. New York Times, 15 August 1980.

37. "Democratic Platform," 1980, p. 11. For impact on candidates, see New York Times, 14 August 1980.

38. Ames, p. 250.

39. Ibid., p. 132.

40. BB Hearing, p. 2

41. Johnson, National Party Platforms, vol. 1, pp. 199, 207.

42. H.R. 11895 and H.J. Res. 579, reported without texts in CR, vol. 80 (1936), pp. 3977, 6677.

43. Testimony on the causes of inflation and related economic matters was offered in support of balanced-budget amendments proposed in S.J. Res. 55 and 92 (1975), reported in BB Hearing. Substantially the same arguments were repeated in a second set of hearings four years later; see U.S. Senate, Committee on the Judiciary, Subcommittee on the Constitution, Hearings: Proposed Constitutional Amendment to Balance the Federal Budget, 1979.

44. CR (daily), 2 April 1979, p. H1870.

45. For discussions of fiscal problems by supporters of a balanced-budget amendment, see BB Hearing and 1979 hearings cited in note 43.

46. Executive Office of the President, Office of Management and Budget, The Budget of the United States Government: Fiscal Year 1979, pp. 11, 35, 233.

47. For 1978 analyses of the California situation and the implications of Proposition 13, see Mervin Field, "Sending a Message: Californians Strike Back," and the editors' interview of Walter Heller and Arthur Burns in "Tax Revolt: The Lady or the Tiger?," Public Opinion, July/August 1978. The long-term advantages and disadvantages of the act were assessed the following year in several non-technical articles, including: Marvin Shapiro, "Proposition 13 Revisited," Public Citizen, Fall 1979, and "Proposition 13: Who Really Won?," Consumer Reports, September 1979. The downgrading of California's general revenue bonds after state taxes, spending, and budget surplus had been reduced was reported in Public Administration Times, 15 February 1980.

48. New York Times, 9 November 1978.

49. From tax table in CR, vol. 96 (1950), p. 732.

50. See, for example, S.J. Res. 149, introduced by Senator William F. Knowland of California to amend the Constitution and establish a 50 percent maximum rate for income taxes. CR, loc. cit. The recommended ceilings generally ranged from 25 percent to 50 percent.

51. BB Hearing, p. 2.

52. The first 22 petitions received by Congress were reproduced in CR (daily), 8 February 1979, pp. S1306-13.

53. CR (daily), 6 March 1979, p. E904.

54. CR (daily), 1 March 1979, p. S1993.

55. A useful summary of the pros and cons of this argument can be found in Congressional Digest, May 1979. Formula approaches to a balanced budget are discussed in U.S. Senate, Committee on the Budget, Hearings on First Concurrent Resolution on the Budget: Fiscal Year 1980, vol. 3, 1979. Testimony of supporters of two constitutional amendments proposed by Senators Carl T. Curtis of Nebraska and Herman Talmadge of Georgia is printed in BB Hearing, which contains no opposition views. Opposing arguments are laid out in a detailed report submitted by Senator Edmund S. Muskie of Maine and printed in CR (daily), 8 March 1979, pp. S2442-51. Both supporters and opponents of a balanced-budget amendment were heard in U.S. Senate, Committee on the Judiciary 1979 hearings cited in note 43. For the kind of brief review offered the average reader of news magazines, see Newsweek, 12 February 1979, p. 28, U.S. News and World Report, 12 February 1979, p. 67, and Time, 9 April 1979, p. 25.

56. Newsweek, loc. cit.

57. Quoted in Congressional Digest, May 1979, p. 146, from testimony before the Subcommittee on the Constitution of the Senate Judiciary Committee, 12 March 1979.

58. The thirtieth petition was submitted by Nevada and was reported in CR (daily), 29 January 1980, p. S548.

59. An examination of the Congressional Record index from 1973 to 1979 reveals that during that period, proposals for constitutional amendments came in biennial waves, rising to new heights at the beginning of each Congress and receding to more modest levels in alternate years. Thus, regardless of subject matter, each odd year produced a hundred or more proposals, while an even year rarely turned up more than a dozen.

The impact made on Congress by the movement for a balanced budget is revealed by the way in which this subject intrudes upon consideration of nonbudgetary matters. In a Senate hearing on a constitutional amendment that would permit "the proposal and enactment of of laws by popular vote," Senator Orin G. Hatch of Utah offered to "bet you money that if we had this, one of the first initiative petitions that would go out all over America would be a petition to balance the budget." U.S. Senate, Committee on the Judiciary, Subcommittee on the Constitution, Voter Initiative Constitutional Amendment: Hearings on S.J. Res. 67, 1977, p. 65.

60. Senate Subcommittee on the Constitution, Hearings, 1979.

61. Washington Post, 19 March 1980. The proposal in question was S.J. Res. 126 sponsored by Senator Dennis DeConcini of Arizona. Eight Democratic members of the committee were joined by Republican Charles Mathias of Mayland to outvote six other Republicans plus Democrats DeConcini and Howell T. Helfin of Utah.

62. CR (daily), 1 April 1980, p. S3325.

# 5

## CONSTITUTIONAL CONVENTION:
## THREAT OR CHALLENGE?

THE DANGERS OF UNPREPAREDNESS

As Everett S. Brown points out in his introduction to the
collected documents on the ratification of the Twenty-First Amendment, political conventions are not new to American voters. The
constitutional convention of 1787 set a pattern for more than three
hundred state conventions, called from time to time over the next
two centuries, to draft or revise state constitutions. [1] Unlike the
1787 convention, which brought together delegates chosen by state
legislatures, the states themselves almost universally adopted a
convention system based on popular election of delegates. Following
this lead, Congress began, over a century and a half ago, to mandate
the use of an elected convention to devise new state constitutions.
The same process has been adopted not only by states seeking admis-
sion to the Union, but also by those undertaking major constitutional
revisions after having achieved statehood. In the 1930s every state
had an opportunity to experiment with another kind of convention
when, for the first time in the history of the Republic, Congress
designated that procedure as the one to be used in ratifying or
rejecting an amendment to repeal prohibition. In a different setting,
the use of party conventions to nominate presidential candidates has
become a practice familiar to the entire nation.
    Despite this not insignificant experience, the only example of
a national gathering for the purpose of modifying the federal constitution occurred in 1787, under conditions vastly different from those
of modern times. The very suggestion that a similar procedure is
again necessary implies both that the demand for a particular change
has reached a critical level, and that Congress is believed to be
either unwilling or incapable of responding to that demand in a way

that will satisfy a widely disaffected public. Rising anger at congressional inaction may lead to a kind of thoughtless, headlong rush into a process for which adequate preparation has not been made. The dangers in such a situation were cited by Common Cause in a 1979 analysis of state petitions for a convention to devise an amendment that would mandate a balanced federal budget.[2] The report's chief complaint was not with the convention system as such, but with the unthinking haste with which most state petitions had been conceived. It noted that "most of the calls for a constitutional convention have passed in legislatures without hearings at which the public could testify and sometimes without even being referred to committees." The report cited as one of the more striking examples of ill-considered action, the approval of a petition by the Maryland legislature without the speaker of that state's House of Representatives knowing what had been done. An investigation of the first 21 state petitions for a balanced-budged amendment demonstrated that: "In only six states were committee reports issued explaining the proposed action; hearings where the public was allowed to testify were held in only six legislatures; in two states no committees considered the petitions before they were passed by the two bodies of the legislature."

The hasty and haphazard approach of state legislatures to the formulation of an amendment petition to Congress is in part a result of the pressures that build behind such emotionally charged issues as abortion, school busing, and budget control. These pressures are generated not only by the rhetoric of the legislative sponsors of the proposals, but also by the often sensational campaigns mounted by private organizations. In fact, the more hotly debated amendments are as likely to originate with special-interest groups as with legislators. Private organizations sponsoring constitutional amendments are admirably suited to the conduct of single-issue campaigns that can be aimed at every legislator in Congress and the 50 states, and simultaneously—or before or later, as tactical considerations dictate—circulated to newspapers, magazines, radio and television stations, and tens of thousands of voters across the country. The selection of targets is aided enormously by the development of computerized mailing lists, scientifically compiled in every conceivable category and sold by commercial firms to anyone with a product or idea to sell. Almost the only limit to the coverage that can be achieved is the cost of mailing lists, of constructing and packaging the message (in appropriately endearing or menacing terms), and of postage. From the frequency with which amendment appeals appear in house and apartment mailboxes, it would seem that substantial funding is available to organizations supporting one or another of the more hotly debated proposals.

As pressure on state legislators increases, the likelihood of dispassionate, unhurried consideration fades. Put in the bluntest possible terms, many state legislators have demonstrated that where proposals for amendments to the federal Constitution are concerned, they simply do not know what they are doing. It is startling, as well as disconcerting, to find that a legislative committee is willing to spend weeks studying the details and implications of a piece of legislation that may affect only part of one state's population, but is unwilling to give similar attention to a proposal that may affect every individual in the nation. Even more depressing is the knowledge that entire state legislatures will pass judgment on a proposed change in the federal Constitution without so much as a routine committee investigation and report. Participants in a 1979 forum on the convention as a procedure for amendment were appalled at the irresponsibility of state legislatures in their simplistic, yes-or-no approach to the issues for which conventions had been requested. As one panelist pointed out, amendments, like the one on budget control designed by the National Taxpayers Union, are adopted by states as their own even though the proposal looks toward a national convention that will simply vote yes or no on the issue, much as the state legislatures had done. [3] Even if the specific source of an amendment cannot be traced to a private organization, the commonality of language in many of the proposals received by Congress from states in all parts of the country suggests a carefully coordinated effort.

The very ease with which prepackaged resolutions are made available to state legislatures encourages fast, unthinking action. A decade before the American Enterprise Institute forum, Senator Millard Tydings recounted this incident to the United States Senate to demonstrate the way in which states are "caught unaware":

> For example, in my own State of Maryland, we did not realize that this back-door attempt to amend the Constitution of the United States by petitioning a constitutional convention had gone so far until about 9 days before the Maryland Legislature was required, by the State constitution, to adjourn. Bills were hastily introduced to repeal the petition which the previous illegally apportioned legislature had approved. In the declining hours of the session, the petition repeal was passed overwhelmingly in the senate. It would have passed the house of delegates. A majority of the members of the house of delegates were cosponsors of the repeal bill. But as the bill reached the floor on the last day of the session the clock ran out. A few more minutes, and the Maryland

Legislature would have rescinded its convention
call. 4

A more general concern of the panelists in the 1979 forum
was the apparent indifference of state legislators to the risks the
nation would face in a careless approach to the convention system.
Gerald Gunther, Stanford University professor of law, expressed it
this way:

> The main danger I see is that the process now under
> way is not a deliberate one. Instead, it is a slowly
> mushrooming, broadening one, ultimately producing
> a kind of convention unanticipated by most of the state
> legislatures that are initiating the process. . . .
>     The states, quite unthinkingly and without consider-
> ation of the implications, have started a process that
> may eventually produce a shock to them and to the
> country. 5

When the moderator, John Charles Daly, recalled the awful
forecast of a magazine writer that a convention might "reinstate
segregation and even slavery, throw out much or all of the Bill of
Rights, eliminate the Fourteenth Amendment's due process clause,
reverse any Supreme Court decision the members didn't like, and
perhaps, for good measure, eliminate the Supreme Court itself,"
the audience responded with laughter. The reaction of University
of Chicago law professor Antonin Scalia was at the same time more
serious and less foreboding. Acknowledging that "All those things
are possible," he nevertheless expressed "no fear that such extreme
proposals would come out of a constitutional convention."6 As the
discussion of risk proceeded, however, Scalia closed in on the basic
theme of convention supporters, saying:

> I am willing to take the chance in having a convention
> despite some doubts that now exist. I am not sure how
> much longer we have. I am not sure how long a people
> can accommodate to directives from a [national] legis-
> lature that it feels is no longer responsive, and to di-
> rectives from a life-tenured judiciary that was never
> meant to be responsive, without ultimately losing its
> will to control its own destiny. 7

Among members of the Congress, the most widely expressed
fear is that a constitutional convention might become a "runaway"
assembly, that it would range far beyond the bounds of its assumed

mission and make multiple changes that might destroy the Constitution as we know it. As early as 1911, when congressional reluctance to heed the demand for popular election of senators spurred some states to petition for a convention, defenders of the status quo did their best to head off adoption of a system they were certain would lead to a far greater disaster than a change in election procedures. A few, like Senator Heyburn of Idaho, whose dire prediction has already been quoted, also resisted action by the Congress to initiate such an amendment. When a direct-election proposal was submitted by Senator George Sutherland of Utah, Heyburn demanded to know the reason for its introduction, asking if anyone thought that election of senators by the people, rather than by state legislatures, would "elevate the standards, intelligence or integrity of the Senate."[8]

## AN ATTEMPT TO CALL A CONVENTION

In the 1960s when 32 state legislatures petitioned Congress for a convention to overturn a series of Supreme Court decisions in which the systems of legislative reapportionment of six states were declared unconsitutional,[9] members of the United States Senate reacted with horror to the states' appeal. Jacob K. Javits of New York decried the convention movement as "ostensibly . . . to revise the reapportionment decision," but really a plot to launch "a broad-scale attack on the Bill of Rights."[10] The debate that followed, on 19 April 1967, was not the first of its kind, but it marked the beginning of a protracted contest of ideas regarding both the wisdom of using the convention system for initiating constitutional changes, and the constitutionality of legislating controls over constitutional conventions. Those in favor of calling a convention in 1967 were led by the Senate's Republican minority leader, Everett Dirksen of Illinois, who had been one of the most outspoken critics of the Supreme Court's decision in the reapportionment cases. Failing to secure Senate support for a congressionally sponsored amendment to overturn that decision, he put his strength behind a drive to call a convention for this purpose. In justification of this effort, Dirksen held that an amendment was essential "to preserve in the States the right to determine their own destinies, as far as their legislatures were concerned." He insisted that in telling the states they could not select one branch of the legislature (invariably the Senate) by districting based on geography, economic interest, or other factors than population, the Supreme Court was usurping a basic state right. He charged opponents of a convention with having "no trust in the people" who would elect the delegates to that body.[11] No sound of snickering was reported in the dry record of the debate when Dirksen

repeated, "I trust the people," or when he referred to Alexander
Hamilton as one of the framers who recognized that there might be
"times when the people may want to have their Constitution amended,
for after all, this is a government of the people." He accused his
opponents of timidity and compared their attitude with that of some
who in 1787 opposed any modification of the Articles of Confederation
with the plea, "Oh, don't touch this holy document." He was supported principally by Roman L. Hruska of Nebraska who argued that,
carried to its logical conclusion, the one-man, one-vote rule would
apply to the United States Senate, "so that there will not be two
Senators to each state but representation by population." Dirksen
left no doubt of his confidence in the outcome of his campaign, concluding with this promise:

> When we get the necessary 34 [state petitions]—and we
> require only two additional States—I shall march in here,
> because this is a matter of the highest privilege, with a
> concurrent resolution and ask that it go to the calendar
> so that it can be considered in due course. [12]

Speaking against "this new assault on the principle of one-man,
one-vote," Republican Senator Javits was joined by such stalwart
Democrats as William Proxmire of Wisconsin, Millard Tydings of
Maryland, and Robert Kennedy of New York. Tydings took the lead
in the April 19 debate, with the avowed purpose of examining the
merits of the demands "calmly . . . before the proponents attempt
to stampede us into convening an ill-considered constitutional convention."[13] His first point of attack was on the states' petitions,
most of which he declared were invalid because they had been submitted by legislatures that, as the Supreme Court had found, were
malapportioned and therefore illegally constituted. Acknowledging
that "a malapportioned legislature may be competent, pending its
reapportionment, to pass legislation generally," Tydings insisted
that "such a legislature has no competence to initiate amendments to
the Constitution to make legal its illegality." As evidence that the
Supreme Court was not alone in calling the states to account for
unconstitutional apportionment systems, he cited cases in Georgia
and Utah in which lower courts had agreed that it was improper for
a malapportioned legislature to propose amendments, either to the
state constitution or the Constitution of the United States, particularly
when the subject was legislative reapportionment.[14] Tydings called
the Senate's attention to a footnote in one court's opinion that observed:

> It is interesting to note the speed by which the last State
> legislature memorialized Congress to call a constitutional

convention to provide for reapportionment "on factors
other than population" . . . compared to the Legislature's hesitancy to properly reapportion under the
mandate of this court. [15]

Tydings charged that of the 29 state legislatures that had petitioned
for an amendment to overturn the reapportionment decision, "23
were unconstitutionally apportioned at the time the petition was
approved, 13 of those 23 legislatures were under court orders to
reapportion, and litigation was pending in the other 10." The petitions, he said, "were passed in haste, without the measured
deliberativeness which should accompany the weighty responsibility
of proposing an amendment to the Constitution of the United States."
Where Dirksen professed full faith in the judgment of "the people,"
Tydings pointed out that the reapportionment of legislatures was
welcomed by the majority of the citizens of the country, but was
most unpopular among the malapportioned state legislatures. It was
the latter, he observed, who were challenging the court's ruling.
His conclusion was that the petitions received from legislatures that
the court had found malapportioned were invalid, and Congress was
entitled to ignore them.

Tydings's second point was that Congress also had the authority
to rule out petitions on the ground that the circumstances leading to
their submission had changed materially. Again he relied on a
decision of the Supreme Court, though his argument was flawed by
a somewhat misleading reference to the court's opinion in Coleman
v. Miller. The court allowed that Congress might consider "a great
variety of relevant conditions, political, social and economic" in
deciding whether or not a later period still reflected the conditions
that gave rise to the petition. Tydings quoted the court's opinion as
though it gave Congress the right to evaluate petitions on the basis
of changing conditions without regard to elapsed time, when in fact
the particular element the court was discussing was that of elapsed
time. [16] Nevertheless, Tydings's point was a telling one, holding
that:

> These petitions must be disregarded because the State
> legislatures which approved them no longer exist. Of
> the 23 malapportioned legislatures which approved
> "factors other than population" petitions, 19 are now
> constitutionally apportioned and elections under the
> new apportionment have been held. In two other states,
> elections are soon to be held.

While supporting Tydings on every count, Proxmire, Kennedy, and

Javits all returned to their common, major fear that although 29 of the 32 petitions proposed limiting the convention to the reapportionment issue, this could not be done because "under the Constitution there is no way in which questions of this kind can be limited to the proposing of only one amendment."[17]

The airing of this problem in the press and in the United States Senate undoubtedly had a dampening effect on the drive for a reapportionment convention. In any event, the filing of a thirty-third petition in 1969 marked the end of this campaign, which was principally the work of the Council of State Governments and a few United States senators led by Dirksen. But the basic problem remained, and a decade later the fires of controversy were rekindled by the more broadly based demand for a balanced-budget convention. Again, many senators reacted negatively. The same fear of an uncontrolled assembly was suggested in many quarters, and when exposed in the media often brought corresponding shudders from the reading or viewing public.[18] Members of Congress were treated to an article reprinted in the Congressional Record from the Seattle Post-Intelligencer of 25 February 1979, which predicted that a constitutional convention would evoke "a battle unroyal, an unleashing of the currents and tensions building these 100 and some years since the civil war."[19]

Those who viewed with alarm the prospect of a runaway convention were neither reassured nor convinced by the conclusions of the American Bar Association (ABA) committee that had studied this problem for two years. In a report dealing principally with legislation to regulate national constitutional conventions, the committee noted the oft-cited "uncharted and dangerous waters." However, it observed that "It is relevant to note in this respect that a similar concern has been expressed about state constitutional conventions but that 184 years' experience at that level furnishes little support to the concern."[20] The committee found that a few state conventions had exceeded the limits placed upon them, though it reported no more recent incident than 1907. The most serious infractions were committed by Kentucky in 1890 and Virginia in 1901. Neither convention undertook to rewrite the entire state constitution, but both made major changes in suffrage that were not ratified by popular referendum as required by the previous constitution. Despite examples of this kind, which under present conditions of universal suffrage and unlimited media coverage are rendered most unlikely, the ABA felt that legislation to regulate a national convention was a practicable as well as necessary method of resolving this problem. The other end of the opinion scale was represented by a legal scholar who, when a convention-control bill was introduced into the Senate, wrote that legislation of this sort would be both unconstitutional and "a national calamity."[21]

The fear of a runaway convention often is based on either the absence of restrictive language in Article V of the federal Constitution or on the history of the 1787 convention. If the wording of Article V and the revolutionary action of the Philadelphia assembly were our only guides, the nightmares they induce would be sufficient to deter even the most courageous pioneers in political experiment. However, there is other evidence to indicate that the use of a national convention now might be attempted without any likelihood that the delegates would attempt to achieve, or could succeed in achieving, objectives other than those for which they were convened.

To begin with, it should be clear that the 1787 convention offers no parallel to twentieth-century conditions. That earlier gathering was openly dedicated to a general review and thorough revision of the then-existing constitution, the Articles of Confederation. Although some state delegations were given instructions regarding the safeguarding of their states' rights, and many fought bitterly against changes that would seriously impair those rights, few took the position that the convention was not free to consider all aspects of the structure and functions of the central government.

By comparison, modern recommendations for a constitutional convention almost invariably focus on specific issues. This inevitably raises the question of whether or not the Constitution permits any controls to be exercised over a convention, regardless of the will of Congress or the stated intention of petitioning state legislatures. As indicated in Chapter 2, the records of the 1787 convention provide no clear-cut answer to this question, as that gathering considered the problem only in discussions of the source and scope of its own authority. The delegates did not pursue the matter in their debates over a new amendment procedure. It is therefore understandable that the point continues to be argued at length in Congress and in professional journals, producing opinions ranging from an unequivocal no to an equally unequivocal yes.


AN ATTEMPT TO ESTABLISH REGULATIONS

When in fall 1967 a subcommittee of the Senate Judiciary Committee held hearings on a bill proposing to establish convention regulations, the arguments offered earlier in that year on the floor of the Senate were renewed, this time with a number of expert witnesses adding their voices to those of the senators.[22] The subcommittee, then known as Subcommittee on Separation of Powers, was composed of Democratic Senators Sam J. Ervin, Jr. of North Carolina (chairman), John L. McClellan of Arkansas, and Quentin N. Burdick of North Dakota, and Republicans Everett McKinley Dirksen of Illinois and Roman L. Hruska of Nebraska. Given this membership and the fact that the bill under consideration had been introduced by Ervin, the hearings offered an interesting opportunity to observe how the shift in focus—from malapportionment petitions to convention controls—would affect the views of participants who previously had addressed themselves to the former issue.

As before, Proxmire and Tydings took the lead in pointing out that few people realized how close the petitioners were to their goal of 34 requests for a convention until that goal had nearly been reached. Proxmire suggested that "one of the prime benefits of an orderly procedure for the calling of a Constitutional Convention should be the notice such a process will provide that State petitions for a Constitutional Convention on a particular subject are mounting and that a Convention is a definite possibility." He credited the press with exposing the quiet campaign of Dirksen, and stated his belief that "the fact that not a single State has acted since that March 17 date [when the story broke in the New York Times] to petition Congress on the subject of reapportionment is eloquent testimony to the importance of complete disclosure in this area."[23]

When Tydings entered the discussion, it was to renew the argument that once a convention is called, no legislative act of Congress can limit what the convention will do. To prove his point he offered in evidence selections from the history of Article V as that section evolved in the 1787 convention.

The hearings at this point are most instructive for the way in which they demonstrate how a single error of fact or logic can lead to an unshakable opinion by the principal advocate of one group that is adopted by other members of the group without further analysis. Tydings's testimony on this point (or, at least, the printed record of his testimony) is sufficiently confused to make it difficult to reduce his argument to a step-by-step analysis with full justice to the senator. Nevertheless, it seems clear that his reasoning was a follows:

1. In Tydings's own words, "the original Madison proposition . . . would have limited it [a convention called under Article V by state petitions] to specific proposals given by Congress."

2. Madison's proposal was opposed by Mason, who argued that it would allow only Congress to propose amendments.

3. Madison's proposal was rejected in favor of the present wording of Article V, which permits either

Congress or a convention to propose amendments.

    4. By rejecting Madison's proposal and approving the present form of Article V, the Philadelphia convention indicated that "if a constitutional convention is called, neither the Congress nor anyone else can restrict it as to what matters it can cover."[24]

    Tydings's basic error was in his initial premise. His statement that Madison's proposal included provision for "a convention called under Article V by state petitions," gives the impression that Madison recommended a national convention as one means of initiating amendments. This is incorrect. The only reference to conventions in Madison's proposal was to state conventions, which he suggested as an alternative to state legislatures for ratifying amendments that had been initiated by Congress.[25]

    Some of the expert witnesses called by the committee, and those whose writings on the subject of a constitutional convention were taken into account, supported the conclusions of Tydings without relying on the senator's tortured construction of the events of 1787. That they were alert to mistakes of this kind is evident, for when a more overt misrepresentation of the convention voting system was offered by Hruska, it was Professor Alexander M. Bickel of Yale University who pointed to the specific error in Hruska's interpretation of Article V.[26] On the question of convention authority, however, Bickel and his Yale colleague, Charles L. Black, Jr., agreed substantially with the view that a convention may not be limited in the matters it considers and, further, that the states "have no authority to require the Congress to call such a convention for the purpose of considering a particular amendment only."[27] On the other hand, Bickel acknowledged the right of Congress "to legislate on the process of amendment by convention and to settle every point not actually settled by Article V of the Constitution itself." Bickel repeatedly sought "a middle ground" between the extremes of an unlimited convention and one restricted to consideration of one amendment only, but he admitted the difficulty of defining the limits in a way that would be appropriate and constitutionally acceptable.[28]

    Professor Wallace Mendelson of the University of Texas took the position that a convention can be limited, contending that the records of 1787 indicate that "no general constitutional revision was contemplated by the convention system." As evidence of the effectiveness of controls, he cited the experience of the state of Tennessee. Out of the same fear of an unlimited convention that afflicts Congress, Tennessee settled on a system "called a 'limited constitutional convention,' a convention limited to the consideration of specific items, with the expectation, of course, that either the legislature or the courts, or both, could enforce the stated limitations upon the convention."29

Other key issues on which both experts and senators expressed a variety of opinions were the way in which conventions should vote, the problem of limited or unlimited choice in convention decisions, and whether or not state or federal executives are entitled to a role in the amendment process. On the first point, Dirksen and Hruska maintained a solid front, as they had done in previous debates on the Senate floor, insisting that because Article V is based on "state action . . . rather than individual action," voting in a convention should be by states, not by individual delegates. In an exchange between Hruska and Proxmire, the former expressed the argument for a unit rule of voting, shading the words of Article V just enough to make his point, and trapping Proxmire into agreement with his representation of Article V, though not to what Proxmire called Hruska's "strict interpretation" of that article. The following brief exchange illustrates again the way in which error—whether inadvertent or purposeful—tends to muddy the waters:

> Senator Hruska. Is that what Article V says? Article V says that any proposal for amendment of the Constitution shall be ratified by the State. It says ratification shall be by three-fourths of the States, three-fourths thereof.

> Senator Proxmire. It does indeed say that, and that is why, with your very narrow and very stringent and strict interpretation, we get away from any opportunity to interpret this particular article to permit more equitable representation. 30

The precise wording of Article V is that amendments shall be valid "when ratified by the legislatures of three fourths of the several States, or by conventions in three fourths thereof."

Except for Hruska and Dirksen, participants in the committee hearings agreed substantially on the need for open debate in conventions, even when the subject matter was limited. Mendelson did not make his position clear on this, ascribing to Alexander Hamilton the notion that a convention is "almost a mechanical device which would simply vote 'yes' or 'no'" on almost any question put before it. 31 Bickel, on the other hand, was strongly of the opinion that constitutional changes are sufficiently important to require thorough review "in a national forum, whether it be Congress or a convention." Because open debate could not be limited by decisions of the states, he declared they "should have no authority to require Congress to submit a given text of a proposed constitutional amendment to a convention to be voted up or down. "[32]

The question of executive participation arose out of a suggestion that the president should not participate even in the consideration of legislation to control the convention process. Both Tydings and Proxmire insisted that the president's approval was necessary, not only to a legislative enactment on this subject, but also to a congressional resolution calling a convention. Proxmire took the further position that the governor of a state was entitled to pass upon the state legislature's petition for a convention. His view was that "If you rule out both the Governor of the State and the President of the United States, it means no official who represents all of the people, either in the country or of the particular State, would have a voice in this very powerful convention." Bickel supported this view, adding, as did Mendelson, a reference to Article I, section 7 of the Constitution as the basis for presidential review. [33]

The give-and-take on the problems of convention controls did not begin with the Senate hearings, as documents attached to those hearings demonstrate; nor did they end with this committee investigation. In other analyses of the convention system, proponents of convention controls have frequently taken the position that logic, rather than legal theory, dictates the need for a convention limited to particular problems on which two-thirds or more of the states demand action. As a 1952 House Judiciary Committee staff report put it:

> The provision [for a constitutional convention under Article V] would be reduced almost to the point of absurdity if Congress were forced to call a general convention to revise the entire Constitution upon the application of 10 States seeking a limit on taxes, 12 States a limit on wives, and . . . more States a limit on the number of new States to be admitted to the Union. [34]

The committee accepted what it called this "sensible rule-of-thumb guide" provided by two experts in constitutional history:

> To be obligatory upon Congress, the applications of the states should be reasonably contemporaneous with one another, for only then would they be persuasive of a real consensus of opinion throughout the nation for holding a convention, and by the same token, they ought to be expressive of similar views respecting the

nature of the amendments to be sought[35] [emphasis
supplied by the committee].

The belief that no limit may be placed on the subject matter of
a convention automatically precludes acceptance of a state's right to
request that a convention be called solely for the purpose of dealing
with a particular problem. As one frequently cited authority puts it:
"In reality, the right of the legislatures is confined to applying for a
convention, and any statement of purposes in their petitions would
be irrelevant as to the scope of powers of the convention."[36] He
applies the same principle to the national legislature, going on to
say:

> Inasmuch as Congress issues the call simply on the
> basis of the application of the state legislatures, there
> would seem to be no warrant for an attempt by Congress
> to limit the changes proposed. The primary and in fact
> sole business of the convention would be to propose
> changes in the Constitution. In this sphere the only
> limitation on it would seem to be Article Five.

That this position does not resolve the question is clear from
the fact that Article V does not mention limitations when it speaks of
a convention. Short of denying the theory of implied powers and the
implications of the "necessary and proper" clause, it is difficult to
insist that complete silence regarding congressional authority in
this one segment of the Constitution indicates an intent to deny Congress any authority in that area. State petitions for a convention
that identify the specific subject of their interest, often indicate
clearly that they neither desire nor expect Congress to authorize
the convention to treat other matters. Of the first 22 applications
for a balanced-budget amendment received by Congress, 15 contained a stipulation that the proposed convention be called "for the
specific and exclusive purpose" of preparing an amendment that
would mandate a balanced federal budget.[37]
As the Supreme Court said more than fifty years ago, Article
V "is intended to invest Congress with a wide range of power in
proposing amendments."[38] Although this view was offered in the
context of a complaint that Congress had acted illegally in placing a
limit on the time permitted states for ratification of the Eighteenth
Amendment, it was a broad response to an equally broad contention
that "Congress has no power to limit the time of deliberation or
otherwise control what legislatures shall do in their deliberation"
[emphasis added]. If the "wide range of power" allows conditions
to be placed on some actions of state legislatures, it must surely

permit the establishment of ground rules for a national convention that cannot come into existence except on the call of Congress. Many states recognized the need for congressional guidance, even in the conduct of state conventions, as early as 1933. In that year, when California petitioned Congress to submit a repeal amendment to state conventions, it also requested that Congress "provide by general law for these conventions," including uniform procedures for nominating and electing delegates.[39] Congress chose not to follow this suggestion, although it did tentatively consider several bills dealing with the subject of convention rules. Nevertheless, when the states passed their own laws calling conventions, 21 of them included in their statutes "a section stating that, if Congress should prescribe the manner in which the conventions should be constituted, the provisions of the state act should be inoperative and officers of the state were authorized and directed to act in obedience to the act of Congress with the same force and effect as if acting under a state statute."[40] Brown cites only one state (New Mexico) as taking the position that Congress had no authority to "usurp" this state's right.

If it is reasonable that the national legislature provide uniform procedures for state conventions, it is practically inevitable that Congress perform the same function in the process of calling a national convention. The question is not whether there should be federal control, but How much federal control?

NOTES

1. ABA, p. 8.
2. Common Cause, "Constitutional Convention is "Great Unknown'," In Common, Winter 1979, pp. 3-6.
3. American Enterprise Institute for Public Policy Research, "A Constitutional Convention: How Well Would It Work?" (transcript of a forum held 23 May 1979), p. 32.
4. CR, vol. 113 (1967), p. 10,106. The reapportionment struggle is discussed later in this chapter.
5. American Enterprise Institute, "A Constitutional Convention," pp. 2-3.
6. Ibid., p. 5.
7. Ibid., p. 18.
8. CR, vol. 46 (1911), p. 2768. The debate was over the introduction of S.J. Res. 134, "proposing an amendment to the Constitution providing that Senators shall be elected by the people of the several States" (ibid., p. 2755). Heyburn's wide-ranging attack was directed not only against the amendment, but against the conven-

tion system as well. He argued that every member of Congress is entitled to vote against a resolution to call a convention, suggesting the possibility that by a negative vote on such a resolution Congress might "legally" evade the clear mandate of Article V (ibid., pp. 2769-73). The sponsor of the innovative electoral reform that aroused Heyburn's ire was the same George Sutherland who, after appointment to the Supreme Court by President Harding, became one of the court's staunchest defenders of Republican economic traditions, and one of the most obdurate foes of President Franklin D. Roosevelt's New Deal.

9. The states whose apportionment systems were successfully challenged by voters were Alabama, Colorado, Delaware, Maryland, New York, and Virginia. The Supreme Court's position is illustrated by its opinion in the Alabama case, Reynolds v. Sims, 377 U.S. 533 (1964). Ground had been broken for the reapportionment cases by the court's landmark decision in Baker v. Carr, 369 U.S. 186 (1962) in which, for the first time, federal courts were declared to have jurisdiction in matters of state systems of legislative apportionment. A year later, in Wesberry v. Sanders, 376 U.S. 1, the Supreme Court handed down its one-man, one-vote ruling, stating: "We hold that, construed in its historical context, the command of Art. I, Sec. 2, that Representatives be chosen 'by the people of the several states' means that as nearly as is practicable one man's vote in a congressional election is to be worth as much as another's." A list of petitions for an amendment to overturn these decisions is included in a Congressional Research Service report, "State Applications to Congress Calling for Conventions to Propose Constitutional Amendments (January, 1963 to April 3, 1973)."

10. CR, vol. 113 (1967), p. 9342.

11. Ibid., p. 10,110.

12. Ibid., p. 10,114. For the complete record of the day's debate, see pp. 10,101-15.

13. Ibid., p. 10,101.

14. The cases cited were Toombs v. Fortson, initially heard by a three-judge federal court and later reviewed by the Supreme Court, 379 U.S. 621 (1965), and Petuskey v. Rampton, 243 F. Supp. 365 (1965).

15. CR, vol. 113, p. 10,102.

16. Cf. Tydings's quotation (ibid., p. 10,103), and the relevant portion of the court's opinion in Coleman v. Miller, 59 Sup. Ct. Reporter 982. Tydings's opponents either did not pick up this discrepancy or did not think it worth pursuing.

17. From Senator Proxmire's address of 19 April 1967, CR, vol. 113, p. 10,103.

18. See, for example, Newsweek, 12 February 1979, p. 28, and readers' responses in the issue of 26 February 1979.

19. CR (daily), 13 March 1979, p. E1060.

20. ABA, p. 7. Errant state conventions are indicated p. 41, n. 14. Evidence that both restricted and unrestricted state conventions were authorized and functioned early in the nation's history is found in the records of those conventions. For example, within 30 years after adoption of the federal Constitution, the New York state legislature called two constitutional conventions, one of limited powers in 1801, another with unlimited authority to revise the state constitution in 1821. On both occasions, delegates abided by the conditions of their assignment. Merrill D. Peterson, ed., Democracy, Liberty, and Property: The State Constitutional Conventions of the 1820's, pp. 127-29. The few changes made by the convention of 1801 are reported in Poore, vol. 2, pp. 1339-40.

21. Charles L. Black, Jr., "Amending the Constitution: A Letter to a Congressman," Yale Law Journal 82 (December 1972): 189-215. Black's letter was sent to House Judiciary Committee chairman Emanuel Celler 28 February 1972, after the Senate had passed a bill to establish procedures for federal constitutional conventions and the House had referred the bill to Celler's committee. The details of the bill are discussed in Chapter 6.

22. FCC Hearings, held October 30 and 31, 1967. The bill in question is examined in detail in Chapter 6.

23. Ibid., p. 8.

24. Ibid., p. 21.

25. The full text of Madison's proposed amendment procedure appears in Chapter 2. It has been checked against Madison's notes as reported in Docs, p. 696 and in Farrand, vol. 2, p. 629, the latter being the source cited by Tydings. Seven errors in the reproduction of a four-line footnote in Farrand indicate either careless clerical work or sloppy typesetting, or both, but these do not account for the more serious misreading of Madison's proposals.

26. FCC Hearings, p. 32.

27. Ibid., p. 61.

28. Ibid., pp. 61-62, 68-69, 73, 77.

29. Ibid., pp. 45-46.

30. Ibid., p. 32.

31. Ibid., p. 52.

32. Ibid., p. 62.

33. Ibid., pp. 24, 45, 63, 65.

34. Quoted in "Procedures for Amending the United States Constitution," prepared in 1965 by Norman J. Small, legislative attorney in the Library of Congress, and printed in FCC Hearings, p. 106.

35. Loc. cit. The source cited in the report is Edwin S. Corwin and Louise Ramsey, "The Constitutional Law of a Constitutional Amendment," Notre Dame Lawyer 26 (1951): 195-96.

36. Orfield, The Amending of the Federal Constitution, p. 45.

37. The phrase "specific and exclusive" or equivalent expressions were included in applications from Alabama, Colorado, Florida, Georgia, Kansas, Louisiana, Maryland, Nebraska, New Mexico, Oklahoma, Oregon, Pennsylvania, South Carolina, Virginia, and Wyoming. Resolutions from the legislatures of these and other states (22 in all) are reprinted in CR (daily), 8 February 1979, pp. S1306-13.

38. Dillon v. Gloss, 256 U.S. 373.

39. Brown, Ratification of the Twenty-first Amendment, p. 515.

40. Loc. cit.

# 6

## A CONSTITUTIONAL CONVENTION
## PROCEDURES ACT

Although Congress refused to assume responsibility for laying down rules for the state conventions to which it referred the Eighteenth Amendment in 1933, it has since considered the matter in terms of a national convention. Perhaps the first serious concern was shown by staff members of the House Judiciary Committee who, in a report analyzing demands for a convention to limit federal taxing power, produced a draft "Constitutional Convention Act of 1953." However, the bill was never introduced.[1] The committee turned an equally deaf ear to convention guidelines proposed in 1957 and 1961.[2]

Not until 1967 did the effort to establish rules for a constitutional convention receive the leadership necessary to gain congressional support. This leadership was supplied by Senator Sam J. Ervin, Jr., of North Carolina. From 1967 until his retirement at the end of 1974, Ervin repeatedly introduced bills to establish regulations for any national constitutional convention that might be called. He was spurred to devise such legislation by his concern that the campaign to overturn the Supreme Court's decisions on state reapportionment might force the calling of a convention with no rules to guide it. Although the required number of 34 state applications never was achieved, Ervin continued to press for a federal constitutional convention procedures act.[3]

Ervin's first bill was introduced August 17, 1967, and two months later was examined by interested senators, consultants, and outside experts during two days of hearings conducted by a subcommittee of the Senate Judiciary Committee.[4] The hearings produced many expressions of support as well as opposition. As indicated in previous chapters, some witnesses questioned the constitutionality of any such legislation. Others approved the bill's objectives but recommended changes in particular provisions. Several aspects of the plan came

101

under sufficiently strong criticism to cause Ervin to revise portions of the bill before introducing it again several years later. The following revisions are revealing in their identification of some of the more sensitive issues raised by the original bill.

| S. 2307 (1967 bill) | S. 1272 (1973 bill) |
|---|---|
| Delegates to be "elected or appointed in the manner provided by State law." | "In each State two delegates shall be elected at large and one delegate . . . from each congressional district." |
| A state's delegates to number "as many . . . as it is entitled to Representatives in Congress." | "as many . . . as it is entitled to Senators and Representatives." |
| In voting, "each State shall have one vote." | "each delegate shall have one vote." |
| Amendments to be proposed "by a majority of the total votes cast." | "by a vote of two-thirds of the total number of delegates." |

Overall, the Ervin bill attempted to deal with the sequence of amendment procedures from adoption by a state legislature of a resolution for a constitutional convention, to ratification of convention proposals by the states. In its final form the measure followed, wherever possible, the safe path of established practice. This accounts for the use of a seven-year time allowance and the plan for determining the size and method of electing state delegations. The most significant departure from tradition was the provision that would permit a state to reverse an earlier decision, whether it be for or against a proposed amendment.

At the time of its final consideration by the Senate, the most up-to-date review of the problem attacked by the Ervin bill was the interim report of the American Bar Association's Special Constitutional Convention Study Committee, which had been issued in August 1972. Because the questions raised by this report go to the heart of the legislative problem, they are used here as a framework for discussion of the bill's provisions.[5] Explanations in support of the bill's position on particular matters, unless otherwise identified, are taken from the Senate Judiciary report on S. 1272.[6]

Q: If the legislatures of two-thirds of the states apply for a convention limited to a specific matter, must Congress call such a convention?

A: Notwithstanding the view of some legal authorities that neither the states nor Congress may limit the scope of a convention, Ervin and the Judiciary Committee held that a request for such a convention was legitimate and Congress was obliged to accede to it. Conceding that neither the courts nor the proposed legislation could force Congress to take this action, the committee felt it was "inconceivable that Congress would refuse to perform its duty" when that duty was clearly covered by every member's oath to support the Constitution.[7]

Q: Is the limitation specified in the states' applications binding on the convention? How much power does Congress have as to the scope of a convention?

A: As indicated earlier, the question of a limited convention goes to the heart of the controversy over the intent of Article V with respect to the function of a constitutional convention. The Judiciary Committee acknowledged this to be "the most vexing" question presented to it. Nevertheless, it held that failure to provide for the establishment of limits on the subject matter of a convention "would be inconsistent with the purposes of Article V and, indeed, would destroy the possibility of the use of the convention method for proposing amendments." The committee argued that the original intent of Article V was to permit both general and special-purpose conventions, and that if states could not propose specific amendments without risking a general constitutional convention, this would make meaningless their right to initiate specific changes by the convention process. "Congress is not required to run such risks in the amendments that it would originate," the committee said, adding, "There is little reason to believe that the states should be expected to do so." Admitting that, once convened, a convention might propose amendments on subjects other than those for which it had been called, the committee believed that such action would be unconstitutional. It suggested what it regarded as the appropriate line of defense against such action by concluding that "neither Congress nor the States would be under any obligation to give consideration to [such] proposals."

Although the ABA's Special Constitutional Convention Study Committee agreed that "Congress has the power to establish procedures governing the calling of a national constitutional convention limited to the subject matter on which the legislatures of two-thirds of the states request a convention,"[8] some authorities took a diametrically opposed view. One of the most vigorous opponents of legislation that would establish convention regulations in advance of any specific need, condemned the bill as unconstitutional on the ground that no Congress has the right to decide for succeeding Congresses the conditions under which a convention may be called.[9] He acknowledged, parenthetically and without suggesting any particular alternative, only that the problems associated with convention procedures "can and should be solved when they arise, by the Congress empowered to solve them, and on the basis of all the factors now unknowable and then existing."[10]

Still another view stressed the need to identify the particular grievances for which a convention is desired, but to leave the convention "free to formulate the best solutions to these grievances." Regulations designed in this fashion were recommended to provide greater protection against excessive limitations by Congress, particularly those intended "to block disfavored amendments."[11]

Q: When is Congress required to call a convention?

A: The committee answered this question in the words of Article V: "The Congress . . . on the application of the legislatures of two-thirds of the several States, shall call a convention for proposing amendments. . . ." It accepted Alexander Hamilton's view that the word "shall" leaves Congress no discretion in the matter, and gave as its opinion that "for Congress to veto State proposals" by failing to call a convention would be "a violation of the Constitution." Section 6 of the Ervin bill provided that as soon as valid applications from two-thirds of the states had been received, Congress was to call a convention by concurrent resolutions of the House and Senate. It further specified that the meeting be convened "not later than one year after adoption of the resolution."

Q: What constitutes a valid application that Congress must count?

A: The bill required that in requesting a convention, a state legislature must follow its normal process for enacting statutes, and must adopt a resolution "stating the nature of the amendment or amendments to be proposed." Within 30 days after enactment, the state's application was to be sent to Congress, accompanied by a certified copy of the resolution exactly as approved by the legislature. Congress was required to keep a record of all requests by subject matter, and whenever it had received applications from two-thirds of the states with respect to the same subject, it was to call a convention for that particular purpose. The Senate committee, dealing with the ticklish problem of how one determines when an application applies to the "same subject" as another application, cited a 1952 report of the House Judiciary Committee as the basis for its conclusion that state applications need not be identical in language. "It should be sufficient," the committee said, "that the States identify a subject or problem, demanding action on it alone."

On this point, the final report of the ABA found the phrase "nature of the amendment or amendments" unclear. But in recommending "improvement and harmonization" of the bill's language in its several references to the subject matter of an amendment without suggesting how that language could be improved, the ABA acknowledged the difficulty of this task. [12]

Q: What is the length of time in which applications for a convention will be counted?

A: Ervin's revised bill adopted for applications the time period that has become traditional as an allowance for ratification: seven years. That is, each application would be effective for seven calendar years after the date it was received by the Congress. At any time that Congress had accumulated applications on any one subject from two-thirds of the states, all applications in that group would remain effective until Congress called a convention. During the 1967 hearings, Senator William Proxmire of Wisconsin was one of several participants who had argued that four years would be adequate, even for states whose legislatures met only every other year. [13] A legal journal note, written after the revised bill had been introduced, supported the four-year period, contending that the rule for ratification is not necessarily appropriate for requesting a constitutional convention. It suggested that "a period of four years, in which advocates of a constitutional convention would have a full chance to mount a campaign, and in which all states would have a second opportunity to evaluate the desirability of a constitutional convention, should be a sufficient amount of time."[14] The Senate committee undoubtedly realized that the opportunity for a second evaluation by legislatures following a biennial schedule depended on their recognition of the problem soon after the first state had submitted its application to Congress. In any case, its response was that a period shorter than seven years "would not afford the States adequate time for debate and deliberation on so fundamental a question as a proposed constitutional amendment. On the other hand, a much longer time . . . would not satisfy the reasoned desire for consensus."

Q: How much power does Congress have as to procedures such as the selection of delegates?

A: The bill provided that each state would elect as many convention delegates as it has representatives in the Congress. Just as senators are elected at large and members of the House of Representatives by districts, so two convention delegates would be elected at large in each state and the remainder would be elected one from each congressional district.

This was one of the provisions with which the ABA took issue directly. Citing Supreme Court decisions establishing the one-person, one-vote principle, it concluded that any other basis for representation in a national convention might be unconstitutional.[15] In effect, it urged a return to Ervin's original proposal, which stipulated that each state would be entitled to as many delegates as it had members in the House of Representatives. The modification that diluted the principle of representation based solely on population had been introduced when the one-state, one-vote provision was dropped. The resulting compromise was another example of the continuing strength of federalism in national politics.

The bill's omission of a nominating procedure was as sensitive of tradition as its rules for election of delegates. While it would have been entirely reasonable to require a uniform nominating procedure for a national convention, any such proposal would undoubtedly meet vigorous objections from states long accustomed to complete autonomy in this area. The only qualification imposed by the bill was that each delegate elected to the convention subscribe to an oath "to refrain from proposing or casting his vote in favor of any proposed amendment . . . relating to any subject which is not named or described in the concurrent resolution of the Congress by which the convention was called."

> Q: What control does Congress have as to the voting requirements at a convention?

A: The bill included only two rules for voting: each delegate would have one vote, and two-thirds of the total number of delegates would be required to approve a proposed amendment to the Constitution. The position of the ABA on this point was that Congress should not impose a voting requirement. It noted the absence of any reference to convention voting in Article V, and the long tradition of conventions deciding their own procedures for voting.[16] However, the consensus in the Senate was that more than a bare majority should be required in matters as important as constitutional amendments, as indicated by Article V requirements for both congressional and state actions to initiate and to ratify amendments.

This reasoning had led Ervin to modify his original bill, which provided for decisions by majority vote. In this section (10(b)) of the bill, Ervin again attempted to reinforce the defense against "wildcat" resolutions by including a sentence saying: "No convention called under this Act may propose any amendment or amendments of a nature different from that stated in the concurrent resolution calling the convention."

Q: May Congress refuse to submit to the states for ratification the product of a constitutional convention?

A: Both the bill and the Senate Judiciary Committee took the position
that Congress has an absolute and unequivocal obligation to submit to
the states for ratification any amendment proposed by a convention
in accordance with the "relevancy" and voting provisions of the bill.
The Judiciary Committee did its best to treat this section of the bill
routinely, referring to the role of Congress as simply "ministerial,"
and attempting to deal casually with Congress's right not to transmit
a proposed amendment to the states "if the convention has exceeded
its authority." Its report went on to point out the protection against
congressional delay or intransigence, citing the provision that if Congress does not adopt within 90 days a resolution either transmitting
or disapproving transmission of the proposed amendment, the speaker
of the House and the president of the Senate are obligated to forward
the proposal to the general services administrator who, in turn, would
be required to forward it to the states for ratification.

This explanation ignored a potentially serious problem. Although
provision is made for ratification by three-fourths of the state legislatures within seven years if Congress does not prescribe otherwise,
a proposal sent to the states without an accompanying resolution of
Congress would leave the states—indeed, the entire country—nervous
and uncertain as to congressional intentions. The mere possibility
that Congress might pass a resolution of disapproval after the proposed
amendment has been forwarded to the states by the general services
administrator, would further strain a situation already demonstrated
to be troublesome by Congress's inability to come to a timely decision
either to support or reject the convention's recommendations. Out-
right rejection would, in all probability, create an even greater degree of political turmoil.

Q: What is the role of the president and the state governors
in the amendment process?

A: Article V of the Constitution makes no provision for action by the
chief executive at either the state or national level. The Ervin bill
confirmed that neither application resolutions by state legislatures
nor ratification actions need the governor's approval. It made no mention of the president. The Judiciary Committee, however, felt it necessary to explain that "after much deliberation," it had concluded that
neither national nor state executives should have a role in the amendment process. There is no indication that the committee considered
the theory of one nineteenth-century writer who held that although
Article V mandates congressional action when requested by two-thirds

of the states, it leaves Congress free to call a convention "on its own motion, by the action of a majority of both houses, followed by the approval of the President."[17] Nor does it appear that the committee took into account the view of a modern legal authority who holds that "the convention call vote of Section 6 of the bill falls squarely under Article I, Section 7, and that the exclusion of the President, and of the possibility of veto, is flatly and indubitably unconstitutional."[18]

The knowledge that such interpretations were possible may account for the committee's lengthy quotation from Edward S. Corwin's analysis of presidential authority under Article I, section 7, clause 3 of the Constitution.[19] (Or it may simply have been trying to cover all bases in its defense of the bill.) As Corwin noted, the issue was settled as early as 1789 when the first ten amendments were referred to the states without having first been submitted to President Washington. This procedure was tested in court when a complaint was filed charging that the Eleventh Amendment was invalid because it had never been submitted to the president for approval as required by Article I, section 7 of the Constitution. The Supreme Court's opinion in that 1798 case is still regarded generally as proscribing presidential action in any part of the amendment process. In the words of Justice Samuel Chase, "The negative of the President applies only to the ordinary cases of legislation. He has nothing to do with the proposition, or adoption, of amendments to the Constitution."[20] Although some scholars deny the applicability of this decision to the action of Congress in calling a convention, there appears to have been no effort to amend either Article I, section 7 or Article V in such a way as to remove all doubt about the matter.

> Q: May a state legislature withdraw an application for a convention once it has been submitted to Congress, or rescind a previous ratification or rejection of a proposed amendment?

A: Despite a century-long history of congressional refusal to accept the right of a state to withdraw or rescind an earlier ratification of an amendment, Senator Ervin correctly anticipated in 1967 what has since become a mounting tide of criticism of this practice. His original bill specified that any state might change its position on a proposed amendment at either the initiation stage of requesting a convention or at the ratification stage, and might do so either by rescinding an earlier approval or by reversing an earlier rejection. This provision received little attention in the 1967 committee hearing,[21] and was retained in each of the several revisions of the Ervin bill. In supporting this provision, the Senate committee in 1973 came to the technically correct but misleading conclusion that "The question of whether a State may rescind an application once made has not been decided by any precedent, nor is there any authority on the question." In the very next breath, the committee acknowledged that "Congress previously has taken the position that having once ratified an amendment, a State may not rescind"—as though there were no connection between the principle of rescission at the ratification stage and at the initiation stage. It went on to insist that "the former ratification rule," which it denied was a precedent, should not be controlling. Rather, it said, the rule should be changed. The committee's further reasoning was confused almost to the point of bumbling, but its objective was clear: a modification of the Constitution should be based on a national consensus that should be measured in terms of the weight of pros and cons at the time consensus is achieved; the weighing of pros and cons will be accurate only if states are permitted to update their positions to reflect current views, and this updating should be permitted in either direction, not limited, as previously, to approval. Despite the potential for argument in favor of established practice, no objection was raised to Ervin's proposal on this point.[22]

If Congress were to adopt this reversal of precedent—and it would be a reversal of precedent, notwithstanding the committee's disclaimer—the change would be made over the bitter opposition of some powerful interest groups, for this change would have an impact beyond the calling of a convention. As this book goes to press, proponents of the Equal Rights Amendment are struggling to secure ratifications from the three additional states needed to reach the required total of 38. Their effort is complicated by the fact that five of the states that initially ratified the amendment have since passed resolutions rescinding that action.[23] Under past practice the rescissions would be ineffective, and if a total of 38 approvals were to reach Congress within the time allowed,[24] those of the rescinding states would be counted in the approval column. But as both the Senate Judiciary Committee and the Supreme Court have stated, Congress is the sole judge of the acceptance or nonacceptance of state actions. Thus a turn in favor of the Ervin formula would spell the death of the Equal Rights Amendment or any other proposal that could not hold the continued support of whatever number of states the Constitution requires for initiation or ratification.

Q: Who is to decide questions of ratification?

A: Only the problem of judicial review keeps this from being a rhetorical question. As indicated above, the Supreme Court has held on a number of occasions that, except for questions as to the meaning of Article V, Congress is the sole judge of all matters concerning the ratification process. The Senate committee supported this position unequivocally, giving courts of the future evidence of its further intention of following standard congressional procedure by adding that "all questions to be resolved by the Congress under the provisions of this measure [the Ervin bill] shall be submitted preliminarily to the Senate and House Judiciary Committees." It hedged only in the sensitive area of state autonomy when it declared: "Of course, Congress has no authority to examine the action of the legislature, except to assure itself that the State has used the procedure specified in section 3." That section mandated that the state follow its normal legislative procedure, excluding submission to the governor of any resolution relating to a constitutional amendment. In effect, the committee was advising the states that it would not use the Supreme Court's position on "political questions,"[25] or the proposed legislation, as a basis for interfering with established state legislative practice.

Where the Ervin bill failed to enlist the support of the ABA was in its extension of the "political question" doctrine to four sections of the bill, each of which contained the statement that the decisions of Congress "shall be binding on all others, including State and Federal courts." The ABA's objection to this aspect of the bill is clear from its final question, which was:

Q: Are issues arising in the convention process justiciable?

A: One of the few generalizations on which all parties can agree is that no one can anticipate all of the problems that might arise in the course of initiating, calling, holding, and acting upon the results of a constitutional convention. Although the Supreme Court has consistently held that there are some questions the political departments of government must resolve, its changing view of what is, and what is not, purely political may widen the opportunities for legal action by persons who feel that a particular aspect of the convention process is illegal or unconstitutional. Assuming that eventually Congress must establish regulations governing constitutional conventions, it is almost inevitable that as soon as there is a need to implement this legislation, one or more of its provisions will be challenged. Even the right of Congress to legislate on this subject may be contested, though the ABA saw no need to question that initial premise of the Ervin bill.

What the ABA and most legal scholars did object to was the bill's attempt to foreclose court review of challenges to state or congressional action in these four areas of the regulations: adoption of a state resolution relating to a proposed amendment (section 3); rescission of a state's application to Congress (section 5b); control of the subject matter of convention proposals (section 10b); and a state's ratification or rejection of an amendment (section 13). It is

not surprising that this aspect of the bill evoked the lengthiest com-
mentary in the American Bar Association report, as well as a suggested addition that would make explicit provision for review by federal
courts.[26]

In addition to the more serious policy problems posed by the
ABA, the Ervin bill took into account a number of less vital but necessary housekeeping questions. These included provisions for federal
financing of convention costs, arranging of meeting facilities by the
General Services Administration, convening and swearing in of delegates by the vice-president of the United States, detailing requirements
for convention recordkeeping and reporting, and defining convention
authority to determine the compensation of convention employees and
to establish rules of procedure consistent with the proposed federal
law.

When submitted to the Senate in 1971, the revised Ervin bill
was passed by a vote of 84-0.[27] When the House failed to act on the
measure, Ervin reintroduced it in 1973 and again won uncontested
approval.[28] Despite overwhelming Senate support for convention
regulations in two successive Congresses, the effort was stopped in
its tracks by the House Committee on the Judiciary, which, both in
1971 and 1973, failed to report out for full House discussion either
the Ervin bill or companion bills offered by House members William L.
Hungate of Missouri and Lawrence J. Hogan of Maryland.

A request for information on the thinking of members of the
House Judiciary Committee brought a variety of responses from representatives who held assignments in that committee from 1971 through
1979. Former Representative Emanuel Celler recalls that "S. 215,
which passed the Senate in the Fall of 1971, raised the specter that
the Constitution would be open to all manner and kind of amendments
despite alleged limiting provisions to the contrary." He also reports
that "as Chairman of the House Judiciary Committee, I requested the
views of the Department of Justice on S. 215 but no comments were
ever filed by the Department with the Committee."[29] Representative
Peter Rodino of New Jersey, who assumed the chairmanship of the
committee after Celler's retirement and held that post in 1973 when
the Ervin bill came up from the second time, offers no explanation
for the committee's action in 1971 when Celler was chairman and
Rodino was second in seniority. He explains that in 1973 and 1974 the
committee was so preoccupied with problems associated with the first
two applications of the Twenty-fifth Amendment (succession to the
presidency and vice-presidency) and with the possible impeachment
of President Richard Nixon, that it had little time for matters "which
were not of some special urgency or priority."[30] Representative
Robert F. Drinan of Massachusetts, who, like Rodino, was on the

committee through the entire period from 1971 to 1979, states that "when the Senate Judiciary was discussing the Constitutional Convention Procedures Bill, there was no discussion of this legislation in the House committee."[31]

The influence of Celler may have been reinforced by a letter from Professor Charles L. Black containing a scathing attack on the Ervin bill, though the former chairman did not refer to Black's letter in his response to an inquiry about this.[32] From the Senate side, former Senator Ervin feels that the House Committee's action was based on an "inexcusable fear that if this bill were enacted the states would call for a constitutional convention every week." He finds this attitude "an absurdity because it is not an easy matter for the states to call for such a convention."[33]

Although Ervin did not succeed in securing congressional acceptance of his proposed rules for constitutional conventions, the effort to establish such controls was continued by others after his retirement. By 1977, however, Senate interest in this legislation had waned, and increasing numbers of House members were introducing bills patterned after Ervin's. One of the more persistent House members was Henry J. Hyde of Illinois who, in May 1977, introduced the first of a succession of bills very like the one approved by the Senate in 1973.[34] Hyde's plan departed significantly from Ervin's only on three points. The first was to permit a convention to propose an amendment by a vote of a simple majority (rather than two-thirds) of all delegates. Second, Hyde made Congress responsible for transmitting proposed amendments directly to the states, rather than through the general services administrator, though he retained the latter as messenger in the event Congress failed to act. Third, the Hyde bill made seven years the absolute limit for ratification of convention proposals, eliminating Ervin's suggestion that Congress or the convention might prescribe a different period for any particular amendment.

Like earlier proposals made in the House of Representatives, Hyde's bill never emerged from committee. Nor did a companion measure, introduced in the Senate by Jesse Helms of North Carolina, fare any better. In 1979 convention bills were reintroduced by several members of the House and, again, by Helms. In the Senate, when Helms's bill failed to gain the attention of the Subcommittee on the Constitution, to which it had been referred, Helms introduced a second bill on the floor of the Senate and asked for its immediate consideration.[35] On objection by subcommittee chairman Birch Bayh, the bill was held at the desk. Although placed on the Senate calendar, it was never scheduled for debate. However, in June Senator Bayh made a commitment to hold hearings the following October, and in August stated that he was "in the process of preparing for those hearings."[36] In response to a written inquiry, Bayh explained his position as follows:

Since the Subcommittee is in the process of holding hearings on the various proposals for a constitutional amendment for a balanced federal budget, I am reluctant to hold hearings simultaneously on the procedures bill in order to avoid these two distinct constitutional questions being drawn irretrievably together.

It is my feeling that the Congress should consider the balanced budget proposals first and, upon thorough investigation and testimony, submit for the consideration of the Judiciary Committee those measures which the majority of the Subcommittee may support. I have always preferred Congressional action to that of a constitutional convention because of the constitutional ambiguities contained in Article V of the Constitution.

As promised, new hearings were held to consider 20 resolutions, all proposing some form of balanced-budget amendment.[37] The arguments at these sessions were largely a rehash of views expressed when the committee took testimony on this same subject in 1975. More than three months after the conclusion of the 1979 hearings, the full Judiciary Committee voted not to support a constitutional amendment, the majority insisting that statutory limitations on spending were preferable to a constitutional mandate. The victory for what was essentially a majority (Democratic) party position was a narrow one—nine votes to eight—with Maryland Republican Charles Mathias joining eight Democrats to overbalance the votes of six Republicans plus Democrats Dennis DeConcini of Arizona and Howell T. Heflin of Alabama.[38] In April 1980, subcommittee chairman Bayh reported that one day of hearings had been held on a constitutional convention procedures act, but that no date had been set for their completion.[39]

Bayh's feeling of uncertainty about the effectiveness of convention controls is expressed in even stronger terms by the chairman of the Senate Judiciary Committee, Edward M. Kennedy of Massachusetts. Unlike Bayh, who voted for the Ervin bill in 1971, Kennedy was absent when that vote was taken and his position "if present" was not announced by Robert C. Byrd of West Virginia, who was then majority whip. Kennedy's present view is that "there are serious and, as yet, unanswered questions on the issue of whether a convention could be so limited [by an act of Congress]." Although he does not rule out the possibility that careful deliberation by constitutional experts may clarify the situation, he feels "It is still debatable whether a convention would have to recognize Congressional efforts to exert any control or influence over the scope of its deliberations."[40] These attitudes of the chairmen of the parent committee and the subcommittee responsible for reviewing legislation on constitutional matters, taken together with the mood of the Senate generally, indicate a sharp retreat from 1971-73, when the Ervin bill sailed through that part of Congress.

In the House, Representative Hyde has pressed Judiciary chairman Rodino and chairman Don Edwards of the Subcommittee on Civil and Constitutional Rights to hold hearings on his latest (1979) bill, H.R. 1964, but with little success. Hyde declared that during the previous Congress, "hearings were not held because the Democratic leadership did not want to provide momentum to the proliferating convention calls." He quoted subcommittee chairman Edwards as saying, "We have never felt it was significant enough to hold hearings," and "anything that encourages this sort of utilization of Article V is unwise."[41] Edwards confirmed this position a short time later in a direct response to Hyde's prodding, asserting that he had polled the subcommittee and found a majority opposed to hearings on the Hyde bill in 1979.[42] In a separate communication, Edwards indicated that his subcommittee staff "has accumulated a substantial amount of research and scholarship on the subject," but he offered no evaluation of the weight of pros and cons suggested by the accumulated data. Holding the door to committee action only slightly ajar, Edwards wrote:

> I have no doubt that should Congress be confronted with the need for calling a constitutional convention, the Subcommittee on Civil and Constitutional Rights and the House Judiciary Committee will be in a position to respond in a timely and appropriate manner. In the meantime, I see no compelling reason—and no consensus exists in my Subcommittee—to anticipate such a situation and pass legislation for which there is no immediate need.[43]

NOTES

1. CR, vol. 122 (1976), p. 8987.
2. Loc. cit.
3. For a summary of the legislative history of the Ervin bill, see CR, vol. 119 (1973), p. 22,733. Ervin's original bill and introductory remarks are reported in CR, vol. 113 (1967), pp. 23,005-7. The text of the bill approved by the Senate for the second time in 1973 is reproduced in full in Appendix B.
4. FCC Hearings, cited in earlier discussions of some of the more controversial questions relating to Article V. From 1967 to

1979, no other proposal to establish convention regulations had a committee hearing in either the Senate or House of Representatives. Senate committee hearings were promised for bills introduced in 1979 but were not held in that year.

5. The questions raised by the American Bar Association in 1972 were reported to the House of Representatives 27 February 1973 by Representative William L. Hungate on the introduction of his bill, which he characterized as "essentially the same as Senator Ervin's" (CR, vol. 119, p. 5495). To avoid confusion or duplication, some multiple-part questions have been divided, and related questions combined. In their final form, the Bar Association questions appear as "Issues Presented" in ABA, p. 5.

6. CR, vol. 119 (1973), pp. 22,732-37.

7. In view of the bitterness of some of the opposition to the convention system, it is well to keep in mind the possibility that, notwithstanding the mandate of Article V, attempts may be made to utilize the defensive strategy hinted at by Senatory Heyburn in 1911. See Chapter 5, note 8.

8. ABA, p. 9.

9. Charles L. Black, Jr., "Amending the Constitution," Yale Law Journal 82 (December 1972): 191-93.

10. Ibid., p. 195. Some years earlier Black had indicated that Congress could hardly call a convention without including "specifications of constituency, mode of election, mandate, majority necessary to 'propose' . . . and other necessary matters as its wisdom guides it." Charles L. Black, Jr., "The Proposed Amendment of Article V: A Threatened Disaster," Yale Law Journal 72 (1963): 964.

11. "Proposed Legislation of the Convention Method of Amending the United States Constitution" (Note), Harvard Law Review 85 (1972): 1631.

12. ABA, p. 18; see also marginal note, p. 47, relating to sec. 2.

13. FCC Hearings, p. 9.

14. "Proposed Legislation," pp. 1620-21.

15. ABA, pp. 34-37.

16. Ibid., pp. 19-20.

17. John A. Jameson, The Constitutional Convention, Its History, Powers and Modes of Proceeding, p. 531. The view expressed by Jameson is contrary to one by James Madison in a 13 January 1789 letter to Thomas Mann Randolph, in which he declared: "If two thirds of the states make application [for a convention] Congress cannot refuse to call one; if not, Congress have no right to take the step." The Papers of James Madison, ed. Robert A. Rutland, vol. 11, p. 417. In any event, the likelihood that Congress would ever use this

method of calling a convention is remote, if for no other reason than that it would invite presidential participation in an Article V proceeding.

18. Black, "Amending the Constitution," p. 209.

19. The committee's source was: Library of Congress, The Constitution of the United States of America: Analysis and Interpretation (1964), pp. 135-36. Black finds Corwin's analysis "murky" ("Amending the Constitution," p. 208), and insists that Hollingsworth v. Virginia does not extend to the calling of a convention.

20. Hollingsworth v. Virginia, 3 Dall. 378. The closest the president ever came to participation in the amendment process was when Abraham Lincoln, for some unexplained reason, signed the congressional proposal for the Thirteenth Amendment. Immediately thereafter the Senate passed a further resolution "stating that the signature was unnecessary and should not be taken as a precedent." William S. Livingston, Federalism and Constitutional Change, p. 215. On one earlier occasion, President Buchanan signed a proposed amendment on slavery, but as the amendment was not ratified the validity of this action never came into question (ABA, p. 44, n. 53).

21. FCC Hearings.

22. A 1979 review of the amending process argues that the possibility of rescission makes each ratification conditional, and declares that any regulation permitting rescission would conflict with the principle of unconditional ratification insisted upon by James Madison. Robert Hajdu and Bruce E. Rosenblum, "The Process of Constitutional Amendment" (Note), Columbia Law Review 79 (1979): 121 and n. 60. The relevant portion of the Madison letter cited by Hajdu and Rosenblum is quoted in Chapter 2. It is remarkable that this legal note, which covers the amendment process in considerable detail and offers extensive documentation for its views, refers to the attempts at regulatory legislation only in a single footnote, and to the ABA study in but two of 367 footnotes.

23. New York Times, 11 March 1979.

24. A further complication was created by the decision of Congress in 1978 to extend the original seven-year ratification period by three additional years.

25. In this connection, the court's changing view of what constitutes a political question is demonstrated by its decision in Baker v. Carr that federal courts may judge the merits of voter challenges to state legislative reapportionment systems.

26. ABA, pp. 20-25, 57. Black ("Amending the Constitution," pp. 210-13) criticizes this aspect of the bill in even stronger terms. Neither of these critics begins to approach the extreme position taken by former Senator Roman L. Hruska, who once declared that the courts could compel Congress to call a convention if enough states requested it, and "should Congress refuse to comply with the writ,

the Court, in enforcing the right, could itself order the Convention."
Hruska's statement is quoted in CR, vol. 122, p. 8988, from a
mimeographed reprint furnished by the senator's office. More specific proposals for judicial review in the amendment process, but
without reference to convention regulations, are offered in Hajdu and
Rosenblum, "The Process of Constitutional Amendment," pp. 160-71.

27. CR, vol. 117, p. 36,804.

28. CR, vol. 119, p. 22,731.

29. Celler to Edel, 10 December 1979.

30. Rodino to Edel, 24 July 1979.

31. Drinan to Edel, 15 August 1979.

32. A similar inquiry addressed to Professor Black elicited
no response. For an earlier reference to Black's letter to Celler,
see supra, Chapter 5, n. 21.

33. Ervin to Edel, 26 June 1979.

34. For the text of the first of three bills introduced by Hyde
in 1977 (H.R. 7008), see CR (daily), 10 May 1977, pp. H4261-62.

35. Bill S. 520, CR (daily), 1 March 1979, p. S1921.

36. Bayh to Edel, 20 August 1979.

37. U.S. Senate, Committee on the Judiciary, Subcommittee
on the Constitution, Hearings on Proposed Constitutional Amendment
to Balance the Federal Budget, 96th Cong., 1st sess., 1979.

38. Washington Post, 19 March 1980.

39. Bayh to Edel, 3 April 1980.

40. Kennedy to Edel, 20 August 1979. One of the sources cited
by Kennedy as the basis for his doubts was Black's article "Amending
the Constitution." See supra, Chapter 5, n. 21.

41. CR (daily), 1 March 1979, p. E819.

42. Edwards to Hyde, 3 August 1979.

43. Edwards to Edel, 16 August 1979.

# 7

## THE ALTERNATIVES

### THE PUBLIC MOOD

When in the early part of the twentieth century the number of
petitions for direct election of senators threatened to force the issue
of a constitutional convention, Congress evaded such a confrontation
by submitting its own resolution to effect this change. More recently,
state legislatures and substantial segments of the public have been
aroused by other issues, most notably those relating to ERA, school
busing, abortion, prayer in public schools, and deficit budgeting.
Only in the case of ERA has Congress responded to the demand for
action by initiating an appropriate amendment and referring it to the
states for ratification by their legislatures. In every other case,
resolutions aimed at establishing the desired policy have been introduced in Congress but have failed to obtain a hearing by either house
or, given a hearing, have not been able to muster the two-thirds
majority necessary to propose an amendment. Each failure has given
rise to a flood of petitions for a constitutional convention.

As dissatisfaction with congressional response to requests for
modification of the Constitution increases, so will the prospect of a
convention. One might assume that Congress always has the alternative of offering its own amendment if and when a convention campaign
reaches what some would consider the stage of "clear and present
danger." But in periods of high emotion, reliance on the availability
of such an alternative may prove a false hope. The attempt to pass
an antibusing amendment in Congress failed when put to a vote, but
this by no means killed enthusiasm for an amendment. Its supporters
will continue to press for amendment via the convention route. A
similar defeat inflicted on a balanced-budget resolution at the committee stage of consideration will not resolve that hotly contested issue.

It is possible that none of the most troublesome problems of the 1970s and 1980s will reach the critical stage at which 34 states demand a constitutional convention. But even if that should be the case, resolution of the question of an uncontrolled convention will only have been deferred. In fact, the drive for an amendment to mandate a balanced federal budget has not abated, as indicated by a survey reported 5 August 1979 in the New York Times, and by the one-vote margin by which such an amendment was defeated in the Senate Judiciary Committee the following year. Although at the state level the Proposition 13 syndrome appears to have passed the crisis stage, the continuing upward price spiral, combined with ever-rising federal budgets, lends credence to the charge that federal deficit spending is the principal reason for the financial woes of millions of Americans. Should this mood continue to spread, there is a very real possibility that Congress will be faced with an accumulation of state petitions that, at least in numerical terms, will meet the Article V requirement for calling a convention. If by that time Congress has passed a Constitutional Convention Procedures Act, it will have a firm basis for deciding either to call a convention with specific limitations imposed under the act, or to determine that, according to guidelines in the act, constitutional requirements have not been met. To make the latter determination in the absence of relevant legislation would create a political storm of far graver proportions than any that can reasonably be expected from a convention.

The current problem is reminiscent of eighteenth- and early nineteenth-century struggles between proponents of strong central government and defenders of states' rights only in the sense that most supporters of amendments to prevent deficit spending, busing, and abortion are also opposed to "big government," and insist on local autonomy in matters such as education and welfare. In other respects the new alignment of forces is rather different. Arrayed on the side of convention regulations are individuals and groups having widely divergent attitudes and objectives. There are those who believe the danger of an unregulated convention is greater than the product of a regulated one. There are also those who see convention regulations as an opening wedge to the convention process by which they hope to effect constitutional changes that will forever limit government's ability to tax, spend, and support activities like busing and abortion.

Against convention regulations are many supporters of social legislation who fear precisely what their ideological opponents hope to gain: a process for establishing constitutional limits on the flexibility of government to deal with social and economic problems as changing conditions require. Some, like Senator Bayh, also feel that

"it will be extremely difficult, if indeed possible, to draft a procedures act to limit any convention to a specific issue." On this
latter point liberals are joined by conservatives of various shades,
many of whom ardently desire the curtailment of federal authority,
but who agree that a convention cannot be controlled, with or without
regulatory legislation. Additionally, some legal authorities oppose
as unconstitutional any legislation that would attempt to find any
future Congress to a specific set of convention regulations.

The new alignment of liberals and conservatives in opposition
to convention regulations reflects a growing fear of the convention
system as such. Less than a decade ago, almost the entire body of
the Senate—liberal and conservative Democrats, liberal and conservative Republicans—supported the Ervin bill. In the relatively
few years since the Senate's last uncontested passage of that bill,
the gathering strength of balanced-budget, antibusing, anti-abortion
forces has turned many Senators (particularly in the liberal wing of
the Democratic party) against the very legislation they supported in
1971 and 1973. Liberals in the House, who seemed indifferent to the
matter of convention regulations in the early 1970s, have since
shown more antagonism than indifference toward proposals of this
sort. Their position is strengthened by the views of influential
private persons who, like Elbridge Gerry, distrust any decision-
making process that does not provide a legislative buffer between
"the people" and the decision.

The character of the debate on this subject makes clear that
the contest over convention regulations turns as much on the
substance of proposed amendments as on opposition to the use of the
convention mode of amendment. Opponents of the convention system
ignore the evidence of successful use of this procedure at the state
level, and deny both the usefulness and constitutionality of the
protections discussed in earlier chapters of this study. To some
extent, the runaway argument appears to serve as a cover for those
whose real fear is a piecemeal rewriting of the Constitution by political conservatives whose power and public following are on the rise.
Their foreboding on this score is understandable, for most of the
amendments pressed upon Congress since the 1960s indicate a conservative reversal of the trend of constitutional change characteristic
of earlier periods. In fact, the case for opposing a convention can
be made in much more explicit terms than most elected officials are
willing to express. Those who argue against the convention system
are content to describe in general terms the danger of an uncontrolled
assembly. The risk can be defined more precisely: a coalition of
like-minded conservative groups may attempt to use a convention
that is called for one purpose to introduce into the Constitution a
whole set of morally and fiscally puritanical principles reminiscent

of those that governed the Massachusetts Bay colony. The overtly close coordination among these groups, and among those who have assumed leadership of their cause in Congress, combines the resources of several amendment campaigns. In 1980 the overall strategy has turned from efforts to influence officials already in office, to a program to elect candidates who would embrace the conservative view and to defeat those who would not. This united front is intent on reversing court decisions and congressional policies by electing representatives who favor balanced budgets, school prayer, elimination of abortion, local control of education, and a concept of law and order that would seriously weaken the protections available to the individual under the present Constitution. Equally important is the candidate's opposition to ERA, most welfare programs, and all taxes beyond those necessary to support a pattern of government sharply reduced in almost all areas except defense.

The success of the so-called New Right was apparent in the overwhelming victory won by Republican candidates in the 1980 elections. Substantial defections among Democratic voters, whose disaffection was due principally to depressed economic conditions, make it difficult to measure the influence of such organizations as the National Conservative Political Action Committee that claim to represent what they call the nation's Moral Majority. Nevertheless, it is significant that many of the liberal Democratic leaders whose defeat had been targeted by those organizations did, in fact, lose their seats in Congress. The most important losses were in the Senate, where majority control of that body and all its committees passed to the Republicans. In the process, Senators Birch Bayh, Frank Church, John C. Culver, and George McGovern were among those replaced by candidates committed to support one or more of the proposals for anti-abortion, antibusing, anti-ERA, pro-prayer, and balanced-budget amendments. Public positions taken by New Right legislators indicate that they will encourage state applications to Congress for a constitutional convention, either as a means of prodding Congress to initiate the desired amendments or as a method of forcing Congress to call a convention.

New Right gains in state legislatures may provide an even greater stimulus to the several campaigns for a constitutional convention. Should these efforts be combined to produce petitions for a convention to deal with a number of problems, rather than just one, the effect would be even more far reaching. There is little doubt that the convening of a multiple-purpose convention would increase substantially the likelihood that such a body would propose a package of "related" amendments ranging far beyond the particular problems specified in state petitions.

A PLAN OF ACTION

This situation poses an agonizing dilemma for one who be-
lieves the convention system is a necessary, democratic alternative
to an intransigent Congress, but who strongly opposes most of the
objectives for which a convention is sought. But whatever may appear to be the horrors of the developing pattern of attack on the
so-called liberal interpretations of the Constitution, a decision on
the desirability of retaining the convention system must be made on
the merits of that system, not on the basis of whether the uses to
which it may be put at a particular point in time are "good" or "bad."

Prior to the 1980 elections, most members of Congress chose
to straddle the issue by avoiding a convention, without declaring
themselves in favor of eliminating the provision in Article V that
provides for such a procedure. In electing to evade the convention
issue, these legislators assumed that a demand for a convention can
always be circumvented by responding, in Representative Don
Edwards's words, "in a timely and appropriate manner." The record
of recent years indicates that this means one of the following actions:
organizing the kind of defeat administered on the House floor to antibusing forces and in the Senate Judiciary Committee to balanced-
budget advocates; acceding to a request for hearings on a constitutional
convention procedures bill, in the hope that the testimony will justify
scrapping the proposed legislation; finding enough petitions invalid
to justify postponing indefinitely a call for a convention; initiating an
amendment for approval in the traditional manner by the House and
Senate; or, as a last resort, calling a convention by means of a
resolution that would incorporate whatever controls are deemed
necessary for that particular occasion.

If the evidence of history were not conclusive, one would need
only an understanding of how Congress works to realize that it is
almost impossible for the members of both houses to recognize and
acknowledge the need for prompt action, much less come to quick
agreement, on any policy questions as emotionally charged as those
for which constitutional conventions have been demanded. To insist
that any one of the five options mentioned above is a realistic alternative to convention regulations worked out in advance, is to indulge in
a variety of domestic brinkmanship that could lead to political turmoil. It is also a denial of the validity of a section of the Constitution
that could be put to better use than at present, when both pro- and
anticonvention forces are using it as a tactical weapon rather than as
a legitimate method of modifying the country's fundamental law.

Put more bluntly, the first question to be faced, and answered,
is whether or not the initiation of constitutional change by convention
is an acceptable procedure. Those who feel it is not should be candid

enough to say so and should be prepared to offer or support an amendment to delete this clause from Article V. Although such a change has been proposed in the past, there is little evidence in Congress of a desire to suggest an amendment that would undoubtedly be interpreted as an effort to deny the established concept of widely based public participation in the determination of public policy. On the other hand, if the convention method is an acceptable option—as argued over two centuries by many political leaders, lawyers, and scholars—then regulations to govern such a convention are essential.

Permanent resolution of the problem could be achieved by an amendment to Article V that would settle the two major points of controversy: limited versus unlimited convention authority, and the role of the president. Such an amendment could stipulate that a congressional resolution relating to the calling of a constitutional convention would (or would not) be subject to presidential approval, and that Congress would be authorized to include in such a resolution rules and regulations for the calling and conduct of the convention that it deemed necessary in the light of requests from state legislatures. This would establish the right of state legislatures to limit their requests to the particular issues they wish considered, and would permit Congress to call either a limited or an unlimited convention as state petitions might indicate. As Chapter 2 demonstrates, such a procedure would be consistent with the most reasonable interpretation of the framers' intent.

The matter of presidential authority could be dealt with more directly by an amendment to Article I that would either deny or confirm the chief executive's power to veto congressional resolutions concerning constitutional amendments and amendment procedures. However, as the more critical problem of convention authority can be resolved only by modification of Article V, it would be more practical to cover both that subject and the matter of the president's role in a single amendment to Article V.

Resolution of these questions by way of a constitutional amendment would undoubtedly require more time than enactment of a law governing constitutional conventions generally. For this reason it might be wise to move simultaneously on an amendment and on statutory regulations, so that the latter could provide temporary protection against an unregulated convention while a consensus is being sought for a constitutional amendment. No one questions the need for the most careful evaluation of each element in any set of convention regulations that may be proposed. Should one or more of the adopted regulations be found inappropriate by a future Congress, there is, on this point at least, no dispute as to the right of each Congress to revise legislation previously enacted. The problem will not be resolved, however, by dogmatic insistence on the questionable position that convention controls designed independently of a convention call would be unconstitutional.

CONCLUSION

At the close of the Philadelphia convention of 1787, more than one delegate expressed both wonder and satisfaction at the group's ability to complete, in so contentious an atmosphere, as formidable task as the design of a new and revolutionary constitution. Benjamin Franklin described the situation best in his closing address to the convention. Admitting the imperfections of the Constitution, he reminded his fellow delegates that:

> . . . when you assemble a number of men to have the advantage of their joint wisdom, you inevitably assemble with those men, all their prejudices, their passions, their errors of opinion, their local interests, and their selfish views. From such an assembly can a perfect production be expected? It therefore astonishes me, Sir, to find this system approaching so near perfection as it does.

Franklin's description of the frailties of any representative group applies with equal force to the Congress, both in his day and ours. If there is any parallel between the postrevolutionary period of American history and the present, it is in the reluctance of the defenders of the status quo to accept any approach to constitutional change that will not guarantee protection against the prejudices, passions, errors of opinion, local interests, and selfish views of convention delegates. These qualities, which are accepted as normal in the conduct of legislative business at every level of American government, are regarded as too dreadful to contemplate when associated with a constitutional convention. It is this fear that raises the most serious barrier to statutory regulations for conventions. The protections such regulations would offer—even the virtual impossibility of gaining the approval of either Congress or three-fourths of the state legislatures for amendments not requested by the states submitting convention petitions—appear unable to still the nightmarish question: What if . . . ?

The longer Congress delays action on convention regulations and/or an amendment to clarify the intent of Article V, the greater will be the danger that the excessive zeal of constitutional reformers, or the excessive protectionism of their opponents, will lead to the very confrontation Congress has so desperately tried to avoid. Sooner

or later the demand for action on a specific measure will produce
pressures that will make calm consideration of amendment procedures impossible. To wait for this moment before facing the
problem, as Congress will discover when the demand for a constitutional convention meets the requirements of Article V, will be to
invite a political storm more threatening than any envisaged by
opponents of conventions and convention regulations.

# APPENDIX A

## APPLICATION FOR A BALANCED-BUDGET CONVENTION

Be it resolved by the legislature of the State of New Mexico:

Whereas, with each passing year this nation becomes more deeply in debt as its expenditures grossly and repeatedly exceed available revenues, so that the public debt now exceeds hundreds of billions of dollars; and

Whereas, the annual federal budget continually demonstrates an unwillingness or inability of both the legislative and executive branches of the federal government to curtail spending to conform to available revenues; and

Whereas, unified budgets do not reflect actual spending because of the exclusion of special outlays which are not included in the budget nor subject to the legal public debt limit; and

Whereas, knowledgeable planning, fiscal prudence and plain good sense require that the budget reflect all federal spending and be in balance; and

Whereas, believing that fiscal irresponsibility at the federal level, with the inflation which results from this policy, is the greatest threat which faces our nation, we firmly believe that constitutional restraint is necessary to bring the fiscal discipline needed to restore financial responsibility; and

Whereas, under article 5 of the constitution of the United States, amendments to the federal constitution may be proposed by the Congress whenever two-thirds of both houses deem it necessary, or on the application of the legislatures of two-thirds of the several states, the Congress shall call a constitutional convention for the purpose of proposing amendments; we believe such action vital;

Now, therefore, be it resolved by the legislature of the State of New Mexico that this body proposes to the Congress of the United States that procedures be instituted in the Congress to add a new article to the constitution of the United States, and that the legislature of the state of New Mexico requests the Congress to prepare and submit to the several states an amendment to the constitution of the United States, requiring in the absence of a national emergency that the total of all federal appropriations made by the Congress for any fiscal year

---

Source: Congressional Record (daily), 8 February 1979, p. S1310.

may not exceed the total of all estimated federal revenues for that fiscal year; and

Be it further resolved that, alternatively, this body makes application and requests that the Congress of the United States call a constitutional convention for the specific and exclusive purpose of proposing an amendment to the constitution requiring in the absence of a national emergency that the total of all federal appropriations made by the Congress for any fiscal year may not exceed the total of all estimated federal revenues for that fiscal year; and

Be it further resolved that this body also proposes that the legislatures of each of the several states comprising the United States apply to the Congress requesting the enactment of an appropriate amendment to the federal constitution; or requiring the Congress to call a constitutional convention for proposing such an amendment to the federal constitution; and

Be it further resolved that copies of this resolution be sent by the secretary of state to the members of New Mexico's delegation to the Congress of the United States; and

Be it further resolved that the secretary of state of this state is directed to send copies of this joint resolution to the secretary of state and presiding officers of both houses of the legislature of each of the other states in the union, the clerk of the United States House of Representatives, Washington, D.C. and the secretary of the United States Senate, Washington, D.C.

# APPENDIX B

FEDERAL CONSTITUTIONAL CONVENTION PROCEDURES ACT
(S. 1272, passed by Senate 9 July 1973)

Be it enacted by the Senate and House of Representatives of the
United States of America in Congress assembled, That this Act may
be cited as the "Federal Constitutional Convention Procedures Act."

APPLICATIONS FOR CONSTITUTIONAL CONVENTION

Sec. 2. The legislature of a State, in making application to the
Congress for a constitutional convention under article V of the Constitution of the United States on and after the enactment of this Act,
shall adopt a resolution pursuant to this Act stating, in substance,
that the legislature requests the calling of a convention for the purpose
of proposing one or more amendments to the Constitution of the United
States and stating the nature of the amendment or amendments to be
proposed.

APPLICATION PROCEDURE

Sec. 3. (a) For the purpose of adopting or rescinding a resolution pursuant to section 2 and section 5, the State legislature shall
follow the rules of procedure that govern the enactment of a statute
by that legislature, but without the need for approval of the legislature's action by the Governor of the State.

(b) Questions concerning the adoption of a State resolution
cognizable under this Act shall be determinable by the Congress of
the United States and its decisions thereon shall be binding on all
others, including State and Federal courts.

TRANSMITTAL OF APPLICATIONS

Sec. 4. (a) Within thirty days after the adoption by the legislature of a State of a resolution to apply for the calling of a constitutional convention, the secretary of state of the State, or if there be

---

Source: Congressional Record, vol. 119 (1973), pp. 22731-32.

no such officer, the person who is charged by the State law with such
function, shall transmit to the Congress of the United States two
copies of the application, one addressed to the President of the
Senate, and one to the Speaker of the House of Representatives.

(b) Each copy of the application so made by any State shall
contain—

    (1)   the title of the resolution;

    (2)   the exact text of the resolution signed by the presiding
officer of each house of the State legislature; and

    (3)   the date on which the legislature adopted the resolu-
tion; and shall be accompanied by a certificate of the
secretary of state of the State, or such other person
as is charged by the State law with such function,
certifying that the application accurately sets forth
the text of the resolution.

(c) Within ten days after receipt of a copy of any such application, the President of the Senate and Speaker of the House of Representatives shall report to the House of which he is presiding officer,
identifying the State making application, the subject of the application,
and the number of States then having made application on such subject.
The President of the Senate and Speaker of the House of Representatives shall jointly cause copies of such application to be sent to the
presiding officer of each house of the legislature of every other State
and to each Member of the Senate and House of Representatives of the
Congress of the United States.

EFFECTIVE PERIOD OF APPLICATION

Sec. 5. (a) An application submitted to the Congress by a State,
unless sooner rescinded by the State legislature, shall remain effective
for seven calendar years after the date it is received by the Congress,
except that whenever within a period of seven calendar years two-
thirds or more of the several States have each submitted an application
calling for a constitutional convention on the same subject all such
applications shall remain in effect until the Congress has taken action
on a concurrent resolution, pursuant to section 6, calling for a constitutional convention.

(b) A State may rescind its application calling for a constitutional convention by adopting and transmitting to the Congress a
resolution of rescission in conformity with the procedure specified in
sections 3 and 4, except that no such rescission shall be effective as
to any valid application made for a constitutional convention upon any
subject after the date on which two-thirds or more of the State

legislatures have valid applications pending before the Congress seeking amendments on the same subject.

(c) Questions concerning the rescission of a State's application shall be determined solely by the Congress of the United States and its decisions shall be binding on all others, including State and Federal courts.

## CALLING OF A CONSTITUTIONAL CONVENTION

Sec. 6. (a) It shall be the duty of the Secretary of the Senate and the Clerk of the House of Representatives to maintain a record of all applications received by the President of the Senate and Speaker of the House of Representatives from States for the calling of a constitutional convention upon each subject. Whenever applications made by two-thirds or more of the States with respect to the same subject have been received, the Secretary and the Clerk shall so report in writing to the officer to whom those applications were transmitted, and such officer thereupon shall announce on the floor of the House of which he is an officer the substance of such report. It shall be the duty of such House to determine that there are in effect valid applications made by two-thirds of the States with respect to the same subject. If either House of the Congress determines, upon a consideration of any such report or of a concurrent resolution agreed to by the other House of the Congress, that there are in effect valid applications made by two-thirds or more of the States for the calling of a constitutional convention upon the same subject, it shall be the duty of that House to agree to a concurrent resolution calling for the convening of a Federal constitutional convention upon that subject. Each such concurrent resolution shall (1) designate the place and time of meeting of the convention, and (2) set forth the nature of the amendment or amendments for the consideration of which the convention is called. A copy of each such concurrent resolution agreed to by both Houses of the Congress shall be transmitted forthwith to the Governor and to the presiding officer of each house of the legislature of each State.

(b) The convention shall be convened not later than one year after adoption of the resolution.

## DELEGATES

Sec. 7. (a) A convention called under this Act shall be composed of as many delegates from each State as it is entitled to Senators and Representatives in Congress. In each State two delegates shall be elected at large and one delegate shall be elected from each congressional district in the manner provided by State law. Any vacancy occurring in a State delegation shall be filled by appointment of the Governor of that State.

(b) The secretary of state of each State, or, if there be no such officer, the person charged by State law to perform such function shall certify to the Vice President of the United States the name of each delegate elected or appointed by the Governor pursuant to this section.

(c) Delegates shall in all cases, except treason, felony, and breach of the peace, be privileged from arrest during their attendance at a session of the convention, and in going to and returning from the same; and for any speech or debate in the convention they shall not be questioned in any other place.

(d) Each delegate shall receive compensation for each day of service and shall be compensated for traveling and related expenses. Provision shall be made therefor in the concurrent resolution calling the convention. The convention shall fix the compensation of employees of the convention.

CONVENING THE CONVENTION

Sec. 8. (a) The Vice President of the United States shall convene the constitutional convention. He shall administer the oath of office of the delegates to the convention and shall preside until the delegates elect a presiding officer who shall preside thereafter. Before taking his seat each delegate shall subscribe to an oath by which he shall be committed during the conduct of the convention to refrain from proposing or casting his vote in favor of any proposed amendment to the Constitution of the United States relating to any subject which is not named or described in the concurrent resolution of the Congress by which the convention was called. Upon the election of permanent officers of the convention, the names of such officers shall be transmitted to the President of the Senate and the Speaker of the House of Representatives by the elected presiding officer of the convention. Further proceedings of the convention shall be conducted in accordance with such rules, not inconsistent with this Act, as the convention may adopt.

(b) There is hereby authorized to be appropriated such sums as may be necessary for the payment of the expenses of the convention.

(c) The Administrator of General Services shall provide such facilities, and the Congress and each executive department and agency shall provide such information and assistance, as the convention may require, upon written request made by the elected presiding officer of the convention.

PROCEDURES OF THE CONVENTION

Sec. 9. (a) In voting on any question before the convention, including the proposal of amendments, each delegate shall have one vote.

(b) The convention shall keep a daily verbatim record of its proceedings and publish the same. The vote of the delegates on any question shall be entered on the record.

(c) The convention shall terminate its proceedings within one year after the date of its first meeting unless the period is extended by the Congress by concurrent resolution.

(d) Within thirty days after the termination of the proceedings of the convention, the presiding officer shall transmit to the Archivist of the United States all records of official proceedings of the convention.

PROPOSAL OF AMENDMENTS

Sec. 10. (a) Except as provided in subsection (b) of this section, a convention called under this Act may propose amendments to the Constitution by a vote of two-thirds of the total number of delegates to the convention.

(b) No convention called under this Act may propose any amendment or amendments of a nature different from that stated in the concurrent resolution calling the convention. Questions arising under this subsection shall be determined solely by the Congress of the United States and its decisions shall be binding on all others, including State and Federal courts.

APPROVAL BY THE CONGRESS AND TRANSMITTAL
TO THE STATES FOR RATIFICATION

Sec. 11. (a) The presiding officer of the convention shall, within thirty days after the termination of its proceedings, submit to the Congress the exact text of any amendment or amendments agreed upon by the convention.

(b) (1) Whenever a constitutional convention called under this Act has transmitted to the Congress a proposed amendment to the Constitution, the President of the Senate and the Speaker of the House of Representatives, acing jointly, shall transmit such amendment to the Administrator of General Services upon the expiration of the first period of ninety days of continuous session of the Congress following the date of receipt of such amendment unless within that period both Houses of the Congress have agreed to (A) a concurrent resolution directing the earlier transmission of such amendment to the Administrator of General Services and specifying in accordance with article V of the Constitution the manner in which such amendment shall be ratified, or (B) a concurrent resolution stating that the Congress disapproves the submission of such proposed amendment to the States because such proposed amendment relates to or includes a subject which differs from or was not included among the subjects named or described in the concurrent resolution of the Congress by which the convention was called, or because the procedures followed by the convention in proposing the amendment were not in substantial conformity with the provisions of this Act. No measure agreed to by the Congress which expresses disapproval of any such proposed amendment for any other reason, or without a statement of any reason, shall relieve the President of the Senate and the Speaker of the House of Representatives of the obligation imposed upon them by the first sentence of this paragraph.

(2) For the purposes of paragraph (1) of this subsection, (A) the continuity of a session of the Congress shall be broken only by an adjournment of the Congress sine die, and (B) the days on which either House is not in session because of an adjournment of more than three days to a day certain shall be excluded in the computation of the period of ninety days.

(c) Upon receipt of any such proposed amendment to the Constitution, the Administrator shall transmit forthwith to each of the several States a duly certified copy thereof, a copy of any concurrent resolution agreed to by both Houses of the Congress which prescribes the time within which and the manner in which such amendment shall be ratified, and a copy of this Act.

RATIFICATION OF PROPOSED AMENDMENTS

Sec. 12. (a) Any amendment proposed by the convention and submitted to the States in accordance with the provisions of this Act shall be valid for all intents and purposes as part of the Constitution of the United States when duly ratified by three-fourths of the States in the manner and within the time specified.

(b) Acts of ratification shall be by convention or by State legislative action as the Congress may direct or as specified in subsection (c) of this section. For the purpose of ratifying proposed amendments transmitted to the States pursuant to this Act the State legislatures shall adopt their own rules of procedure. Any State action ratifying a proposed amendment to the Constitution shall be valid without the assent of the Governor of the State.

(c) Except as otherwise prescribed by concurrent resolution of the Congress, any proposed amendment to the Constitution shall become valid when ratified by the legislatures of three-fourths of the several States within seven years from the date of the submission thereof to the States, or within such other period of time as may be prescribed by such proposed amendment.

(d) The secretary of state of the State, or if there be no such officer, the person who is charged by State law with such function, shall transmit a certified copy of the State action ratifying any proposed amendment to the Administrator of General Services.

## RESCISSION OF RATIFICATIONS

Sec. 13. (a) Any State may rescind its ratification of a proposed amendment by the same process by which it ratified the proposed amendment, except that no State may rescind when there are existing valid ratifications of such amendment by three-fourths of the States.

(b) Any state may ratify a proposed amendment even though it previously may have rejected the same proposal.

(c) Questions concerning State ratification or rejection of amendments proposed to the Constitution of the United States, shall be determined solely by the Congress of the United States, and its decisions shall be binding on all others, including State and Federal courts.

## PROCLAMATION OF CONSTITUTIONAL AMENDMENTS

Sec. 14. The Administrator of General Services, when three-fourths of the several States have ratified a proposed amendment to the Constitution of the United States, shall issue a proclamation that the amendment is part of the Constitution of the United States.

## EFFECTIVE DATE OF AMENDMENTS

Sec. 15. An amendment proposed to the Constitution of the United States shall be effective from the date specified therein or, if no date is specified, then on the date on which the last State necessary to constitute three-fourths of the States of the United States, as provided for in article V, has ratified the same.

# BIBLIOGRAPHY

UNITED STATES GOVERNMENT
DOCUMENTS AND PUBLICATIONS

Congressional Record (volumes as cited in notes).

Executive Office of the President, Office of Management and Budget.
The Budget of the United States Government: Fiscal Year 1979.
Washington, D.C.: Government Printing Office, 1978.

General Services Administration, Office of the Federal Register.
Documents of ratification of the Equal Rights Amendment.

House of Representatives, Committee on the Judiciary, Subcommittee
on Civil and Constitutional Rights. Equal Rights Amendment
Extension: Hearings on H.J. Res. 638, 95th Cong., 1st and 2d
sess., 1977-78.

Library of Congress. Paul H. Smith Letters of Delegates to Congress
1774-1789. 4 vols. to date. Washington, D.C.: Government
Printing Office, 1976-79.

____. Legislative Reference Service. The Constitution of the United
States of America: Analysis and Interpretation. Washington, D.C.:
Government Printing Office, 1953.

____. Documents Illustrative of the Formation of the Union of Ameri-
can States. Washington, D.C.: Government Printing Office, 1927.

____. Congressional Research Service. "State Applications to
Congress Calling for Conventions to Propose Constitutional
Amendments (January, 1963 to April 3, 1973)." Mimeographed.

____. "State Applications to Congress Calling for Conventions to
Propose Constitutional Amendments Received from June 9, 1973
through March 24, 1976." Mimeographed.

Poore, Ben Perley, comp. The Federal and State Constitutions,
Colonial Charters, and Other Organic Laws of the United States.
2 vols. Washington, D.C.: Government Printing Office, 1878.

Senate, Committee on the Budget. First Concurrent Resolution on the Budget—Fiscal Year 1980: Hearings, 3 vols., 96th Cong., 1st sess., 1979.

_____, Committee on the Judiciary, Subcommittee on the Constitution. Proposed Constitutional Amendment to Balance the Federal Budget: Hearings on S.J. Res. 2, 96th Cong., 1st sess., 1979.

_____, Voter Initiative Constitutional Amendment: Hearings on S.J. Res. 67, 95th Cong., 1st sess., 1977.

_____, Committee on the Judiciary, Subcommittee on Constitutional Amendments. Balancing the Budget: Hearing on S.J. Res. 55 and 93, 94th Cong., 1st sess., 1975.

_____, Committee on the Judiciary, Subcommittee on Separation of Powers. Federal Constitutional Convention: Hearings on S. 2307, 90th Cong., 1st sess., 1967.

United States Code (volumes as cited in notes).

United States Reports (volumes as cited in notes; see separate list of Supreme Court cases, this bibliography).

## SUPREME COURT CASES

Baker v. Carr, 369 U.S. 186 (1962).

Brown v. Board of Education, 347 U.S. 483 (1954); 349 U.S. 294 (1955).

Chandler v. Wise, 307 U.S. 474 (1939).

Coleman v. Miller, 307 U.S. 433 (1939).

Dillon v. Gloss, 256 U.S. 368 (1921).

Engel v. Vitale, 370 U.S. 421 (1962).

Fairchild v. Hughes, 258 U.S. 126 (1922).

Hawke v. Smith, 253 U.S. 221 (1920).

Hollingsworth v. Virginia, 3 Dall. 378 (1798).

Leser v. Garnett, 258 U.S. 130 (1922).

Reynolds v. Sims, 377 U.S. 533 (1964).

Rhode Island v. Palmer, 253 U.S. 350 (1920).

Roe v. Wade, 410 U.S. 113 (1973).

School District of Abington Township v. Schempp, 374 U.S. 203 (1963).

Swann v. Charlotte-Mecklenburg County Board of Education, 402 U.S. 1 (1971).

United States v. Sprague, 282 U.S. 716 (1931).

Wesberry v. Sanders, 376 U.S. 1 (1963).

Whitehill v. Elkins, 389 U.S. 54 (1967).

PERSONAL CORRESPONDENCE FROM MEMBERS OF THE CONGRESS (Judiciary committee membership since 1971 noted)

Bayh, Birch, Democratic senator from Indiana (committee member, 1971-80; chairman, Subcommittee on Constitutional Amendments, 1971-78; chairman, Subcommittee on the Constitution, 1979-80), letters of 20 August 1979 and 3 April 1980.

Celler, Emanuel, Democratic representative from New York (committee chairman, 1971-72), letter of 10 December 1979.

DeConcini, Dennis, Democratic senator from Arizona (committee member, 1977-80), letter of 6 September 1979.

Dole, Robert J., Republican senator from Kansas (committee member, 1979-80), letter of 28 August 1979.

Drinan, Robert F., Democratic representative from Massachusetts (committee member, 1971-80), letter of 15 August 1979.

Edwards, Don, Democratic representative from California (committee member, 1971-80; chairman, Subcommittee on Civil and Constitutional Rights, 1974-80), letters of 3 August 1979 to Henry J. Hyde and 6 August 1979 to the author.

Ertel, Allen E. , Democratic representative from Pennsylvania, letter of 6 July 1979.

Ervin, Sam J. , Jr. , Democratic senator from North Carolina (committee member, 1971-74; chairman, Subcommittee on Separation of Powers, 1971-74), letter of 26 June 1979.

Heinz, H. John, III, Republican senator from Pennsylvania, letter of 30 March 1979.

Hyde, Henry J. , Republican representative from Illinois (committee member, 1975-80; ranking minority member, Subcommittee on Civil and Constitutional Rights, 1979-80), undated office memorandum, August (?) 1979.

Kennedy, Edward M. , Democratic senator from Massachusetts (committee member, 1971-80; committee chairman, 1979-80), letter of 30 August 1979.

Rodino, Peter W. , Jr. , Democratic representative from New Jersey (committee member, 1971-80; committee chairman, 1973-80), letter of 24 July 1979.

Schweiker, Richard S. , Republican senator from Pennsylvania, letter of 25 May 1979.

Thurmond, Strom, Republican senator from South Carolina (committee member, 1971-80; ranking minority member, 1977-80), letter of 2 October 1979.


GENERAL

American Bar Association, Special Constitutional Convention Study Committee. "Amendment of the Constitution by the Convention Method under Article V. " Chicago, 1973.

American Enterprise Institute for Public Policy Research. "A Constitutional Convention: How Well Would It Work?" Transcript of a forum held 23 May 1979.

Ames, Herman V. Proposed Amendments to the Constitution of the United States during the First Century of Its History. Reprint. New York: Burt Franklin, 1970.

Bethea, Andrew J. The Contribution of Charles Pinckney to the Formation of the American Union. Richmond, Va.: Garrett and Massie, 1937.

Billias, George Athan. Elbridge Gerry, Founding Father and Republican Statesman. New York: McGraw-Hill, 1976.

Black, Charles L., Jr. "Amending the Constitution: A Letter to a Congressman." Yale Law Journal 82 (December 1972): 189-215.

____. "The Proposed Amendment of Article V: A Threatened Disaster." Yale Law Journal 72 (April 1963): 957-66.

Brown, Everett Somerville. Ratification of the Twenty-first Amendment to the Constitution of the United States. Reprint. New York: Da Capo Press, 1970.

Commager, Henry Steele, ed. Documents of American History. 2d ed. New York: F. S. Crofts, 1940.

Common Cause. "Constitutional Convention is 'Great Unknown'." In Common, Winter 1979, pp. 3-6.

Constitutions of the United States, National and State. 7 vols. Published for the Legislative Drafting Research Fund of Columbia University. Dobbs Ferry, N.Y.: Oceania Publications, 1978-79.

Council of State Governments. "Amending the Constitution to Strengthen the States in the Federal System." State Government 36 (Winter 1963): 10-15.

Current, June 1979.

Debates and Proceedings in the Convention of the Commonwealth of Massachusetts, Held in the Year 1788. Boston: William White, 1856.

"Debt Ceiling Bill and Budget-Balancing Efforts." Congressional Digest, May 1979, pp. 129-30.

Elliot, Jonathan. The Debates in the Several State Conventions on the Adoption of the Federal Constitution, as Recommended by the General Convention at Philadelphia in 1787. 5 vols. Philadelphia: J. B. Lippincott, 1891.

Farrand, Max, ed. The Records of the Federal Convention of 1787. 4 vols. New Haven, Conn.: Yale University Press, 1923.

Federalist. New York: Modern Library, 1937.

Field, Mervin. "Sending a Message: Californians Strike Back." Public Opinion, July/August 1978, pp. 3-7.

Ford, Paul Leicester, ed. Essays on the Constitution of the United States. Brooklyn, N.Y.: Historical Printing Club, 1892.

Freeman, Douglas Southall. George Washington: A Biography. 7 vols. New York: Charles Scribner's Sons, 1948-54.

Gunther, Gerald. "Constitutional Brinkmanship: Stumbling toward a Convention." American Bar Association Journal 65 (1979): 1046-49.

Hajdu, Robert, and Bruce E. Rosenblum. "The Process of Constitutional Amendment" (Note). Columbia Law Review 79 (1979): 106-72.

Hamilton, Alexander. The Papers of Alexander Hamilton. Edited by Harold C. Syrett. 26 vols. New York: Columbia University Press, 1961-79.

Jameson, J. Franklin. Essays in the Constitutional History of the United States in the Formative Period 1775-1789. Boston: Houghton Mifflin, 1889.

Jameson, John A. The Constitutional Convention, Its History, Powers and Modes of Proceeding. New York: Scribner, 1867.

Jefferson, Thomas. The Papers of Thomas Jefferson. Edited by Julian P. Boyd. 19 vols. Princeton, N.J.: Princeton University Press, 1950-74.

Johnson, Donald Bruce, comp. National Party Platforms. 2 vols. Urbana, Ill.: University of Chicago Press, 1978.

Lincoln, Abraham. The Collected Works of Abraham Lincoln. Edited by Ray P. Basler. 8 vols. New Brunswick, N.J.: Rutgers University Press, 1953.

Livingston, William S. Federalism and Constitutional Change. Oxford: Clarendon Press, 1956.

Long, Breckinridge. Genesis of the Constitution of the United States of America. New York: Macmillan, 1926.

Madison, James. The Papers of James Madison. Vols. 1-7 edited by William T. Hutchinson and William M. E. Rachal; vols. 8-12 edited by Robert A. Rutland, William M. E. Rachal, and Charles F. Hobson. Chicago: University of Chicago Press (vols. 1-10), 1962-77. Charlottesville, Va.: University Press of Virginia (vols. 11-12), 1977-79.

Miller, Helen Hill. George Mason, Gentleman Revolutionary. Chapel Hill, N.C.: University of North Carolina Press, 1975.

Miller, Maxwell A. "The ERA Ratification Game: Changing the Rules at Halftime." Student Lawyer, January 1980, p. 11.

Mintz, Max M. Gouverneur Morris and the American Revolution. Norman, Okla.: University of Oklahoma Press, 1970.

Musmanno, M. A. Proposed Amendments to the Constitution. Washington: U.S. Government Printing Office, 1929.

Newsweek, 12 February 1979.

New York Times (as cited in notes).

Noonan, John T., Jr. "The Convention Method of Constitutional Amendment: Its Meaning, Usefulness and Wisdom." Congressional Record (daily), 3 May 1979, p. S5349.

Orfield, Lester B. The Amending of the Federal Constitution. Reprint. New York: Da Capo Press, 1971.

Peterson, Merrill D., ed. Democracy, Liberty, and Property, The State Constitutional Conventions of the 1820's. New York: Bobbs-Merrill, 1966.

"Proposed Constitutional Amendments to Require Balanced Budgets." Congressional Digest, May 1979, pp. 131-59.

"Proposed Legislation on the Convention Method of Amending the United States Constitution" (Note). Harvard Law Review 85 (1972): 1612-48.

"Proposition 13: Who Really Won?" Consumer Reports, September 1979.

Public Administration Times, 15 February 1980.

Public Opinion Quarterly, 1975-80.

Republican National Committee. Republican Platform. 1980.

Shapiro, Marvin. "Proposition 13 Revisited." Public Citizen, Fall 1979, p. 6.

"Should a Constitutional Amendment Be Adopted to Require Balanced Federal Budget?" Congressional Digest, May 1979, pp. 138-59.

Stasny, James. "Toward a Civically Militant Electorate: A National Constitutional Convention." Congressional Record 122 (1976): 8985-92.

_____. "State Applications for a Convention to Amend the Federal Constitution, January 1974—September 1977: Compilation and Comment." Congressional Record (daily), 2 November 1977, pp. S18494-99.

"State Action toward a Constitutional Convention." Congressional Digest, May 1979, p. 134.

Stille, Charles J. The Life and Times of John Dickinson. Philadelphia: J. B. Lippincott, 1891.

"Summary of Proposed Constitutional Amendments." Congressional Digest, May 1979, pp. 136-37.

Time, 9 April 1979.

U.S. News and World Report, 12 February 1979.

Washington Post (as cited in notes).

Wattenberg, Ben, ed. "Tax Revolt: The Lady or the Tiger?" Public Opinion, July/August 1978, pp. 8-14.

Wells, William V. The Life and Public Services of Samuel Adams. 3 vols. Boston: Little, Brown, 1865.

# INDEX

146

Council of Censors, Pennsylvania, 7
Council of Revision, 34
Council of State Governments, 11, 90
Crane, Philip M., 62
Crisp, Mary, 69
Culver, John C., 122

Daly, John Charles, 86
Davis, Garrett, 9, 10
Declaration of Independence, 6
declaration of rights, 5-6
DeConcini, Dennis, 73-74, 113
Delaware, constitution of, 2, 6, 8; position on national convention, 9, 21
democracy, 23
Democratic party platform (see abortion, balanced-budget amendment, equal rights amendment, prayer in public schools, school busing)
depression of 1930s, 71
desegregation (see school busing)
Dickinson, John, 19-20
Dirksen, Everett McKinley, 87, 90, 92, 94
discharge petition, use of, 61, 62
Douglas, William O., 54
Drinan, Robert F., 111

education (see prayer in public schools, school busing)
Edwards, Don, 114, 123
Elliot, Jonathan, 37
Ellsworth, Oliver, 27
Equal Rights Amendment (ERA), 67-69, 109, 119; extension of ratification period for, 46; religious issue and, 68; suit to prevent ratification of, 46, 48

Ervin, Sam J., Jr., 25, 60, 91-92, 101, 112
Ervin bill (see Federal Constitutional Convention Procedures Act)

family planning, 64 (see also abortion)
Farrand, Max, 27
Federal Constitutional Convention Procedures Act, 101-14, 120
Federalist, 37
first amendment (see prayer in public schools)
fourteenth amendment: abortion right protected by, 63; ratified despite rescissions, 48
Franklin, Benjamin, 19, 125
Fundamental Orders of Connecticut, 2

Galloway, Joseph, 19
General Services Administrator, 107, 112
George III (King of England), 19
Georgia, constitution of, 2, 7, 8; petitions for budget-surplus amendment, 70
Gerry, Elbridge, 4, 23-24, 26, 27-28, 29, 34
Gorham, Nathaniel, 27
governor, role of in ratification procedure, 95, 107
Grant, Ulysses S., 70
Gudger, Lamar, 62
Gunther, Gerald, 86

Hamilton, Alexander, 4, 22, 28-29, 31-34
Hartford convention, 2
Heflin, Howell T., 113
Helms, Jesse, 62, 64, 112
"Helms amendment" (see prayer in public schools)
Henderson, John B., 10

Henry, Patrick, 21, 31
Herrick, Ebenezer, 9
Heyburn, Weldon B., 25, 87
Hogan, Lawrence J., 64, 111
House judiciary committee, and prayer in public schools, 62; and Federal Constitutional Convention Procedures Act, 111-12
Hruska, Roman L., 88, 92, 93-94
Hungate, William L., 111
Hyde, Henry J., 112, 114

Idaho, ratifies after rejection, 47; sues to block ERA, 46, 48, 68
Igoe, William L., 11
income tax, 73
Indiana, petition on abortion, 64
item veto, 70

Jackson, Henry M., 60
Jarvis, Howard, 74
Javits, Jacob K., 87-88
Jefferson, Thomas, 7-8
Johnson, William Samuel, 29
judiciary, U.S., 36 (see also Supreme Court decisions)
Judiciary committee (see House Judiciary committee, Senate Judiciary committee)

Kansas, challenge of child labor amendment by, 47
Kennedy, Edward M., 113
Kennedy, Robert, 88, 89-90
Kentucky, constitution of, 90
King, Rufus, 29
Knutson, Harold, 71

legislature, national (see Congress, Continental Congress)
legislature, state: as originator of constitutional amendments,

6-7; as originator of state constitution, 2-3, 6; authority to call state convention, 7
Lincoln, Abraham, 12
Louisiana, constitution of, 8; opposes school busing, 60

McClellan, John L., 91
McFarlane, W. D., 71
McGovern, George, 122
Madison, James, 4, 22-24, 28-29, 30, 31-32, 36
"March for Life," 65
Maryland, constitution of, 2, 5, 6; petitions for balanced-budget amendment, 84, 85
Mason, George, 4, 23-24, 26, 29
Massachusetts, constitution of, 2-3, 7
Massachusetts Bay colony, 2
Mathias, Charles, 113
Mendelson, Wallace, 25, 94-95
Mississippi, opposes school busing, 60
Mormon Church, 68
Morris, Gouverneur, 21, 24, 29-30, 37

National Abortion Rights League, 67
National Committee for a Constitutional Amendment, 12
National Conservative Political Action Committee, 122
national debt, 71-72
National Taxpayers Union, 85
New England Federation, 2
New Hampshire, constitution of, 2, 8
New Jersey, constitution of, 2
New Jersey plan for federal constitution, 22 (see also Patterson, William)
New Right, 122

New York, proposes national
convention, 9
New York Times, 92
Nicholas, Wilson, 31
Nixon, Richard M., 60-61
North Carolina, constitution of,
2

Ohio, constitution of, 8; holds
referendum on eighteenth
amendment, 44
Owen, Robert L., 11

Patterson, William, 22; and plan
for federal constitution, 33
Pennsylvania, constitution of, 2,
7; council of censors, 7
people, as source of authority
(see popular sovereignty)
petitions for constitutional
amendment: character of,
84-86; from private organizations, 84-85 (see also
abortion, balanced-budget
amendment, prayer in public
schools, reapportionment
cases, school busing)
Philadelphia convention (see
Constitutional Convention of
1787)
Pinckney, Charles, 22, 23, 26,
33
political questions, and the
Supreme Court, 48, 54; in
Ervin bill, 110-11
popular sovereignty, 5-7, 44
Porter, Charles H., 10
prayer in public schools, 61-62,
119
President, role in amendment
process, 33-38, 95, 107-08,
124 (see also Article I)
presidential succession, 59
privacy, right of, 63, 66

prohibition (see eighteenth amendment)
"Proposition 13," 72, 120
Proxmire, William, 88, 89-90,
92, 94-95, 105
public opinion, on abortion, 60;
on government fiscal policy, 60
Public Opinion Quarterly, 60

Randolph, Edmund, 4, 7-8, 22-
23, 24, 26-27, 35, 36
Randolph, John, 7
ratification procedure under
Article V: by state conventions,
1, 23, 51-52; by state legislatures, 23; conditional, 46;
time allowed for, 45-46 (see
also amendment procedure)
reapportionment cases, 87
rescission of ratification, 47-48,
108-09; Democratic party
position on, 69; of ERA, 47,
48; of fourteenth amendment,
48; Republican party position
on, 69 (see also amendment
procedure, ratification procedure)
referendum, national, 11
referendum, state: and amendments to U.S. Constitution, 44;
in Kentucky, 90; in Virginia,
90; in Ohio, 44
religion, in school prayer dispute,
63; in ERA campaign, 68
Republican party platform (see
abortion, balanced budget
amendment, equal rights amendment, prayer in public schools,
school busing)
revolution, right of, 6
Rhode Island, constitution of, 2;
fear of strong central government, 21, 24
right-to-life amendment (see
abortion)

149

Rodino, Peter W., Jr., 111, 114
Rodney, Caesar, 3
Roe v. Wade, 63-64
Rutledge, John, 24, 27, 28-29

Scalia, Antonin, 86
school busing, 13, 60-61, 119
Seattle Post-Intelligencer, 90
Senate, president of, 107; representation in, 24, 30, 45
Senate Finance committee, 72
Senate Judiciary committee, 75, 102-13 passim, 120
senators, direct election of, 10, 13, 119
Separation of Powers, Senate subcommittee on, 91-92
Sherman, Roger, 24, 29-30, 36
slavery, 22, 23-24
South Carolina, constitution of, 8; proposes national convention, 9
South Dakota, petition for anti-abortion amendment, 65; resolution to nullify ratification of ERA, 46
Speaker, U.S. House of Representatives, 107
state constitutions (see individual state listings, amendment procedure in state constitutions)
state conventions (see constitutional conventions, state)
states' rights, 9, 24, 28, 29-31, 87, 91
Stennis, John C., 74-75
Student Transportation Moratorium Act, 60-61
suffrage, 7-8, 22; for women, 10, 22; in twentieth century, 59
Supreme Court decisions: affecting Article V, 43-55; on abortion, 63-64; on limits

imposed by states, 54; on limits of courts' jurisdiction, 54; on political decisions, 48, 54; on prayer in public schools, 61; on ratification after rejection, 47, 110; on reasonable time for ratification, 45; on school busing, 60; on state referenda in ratification process, 44; on two-thirds voting rule, 53
Sutherland, George, 87

term of office, presidential, 59; legislative, 59
Texas, and balanced-budget amendment, 73; ratification by after rejection, 47
two-thirds rule, in Congress, 45, 53
Tydings, Joseph D., 25
Tydings, Millard, 85, 88-89, 92-93

Ullman, Al, 72
Unit rule, in constitutional convention, 94, 102

Vallandigham, Clement L., 9
veto (see President, role in amendment process)
Virginia, constitution of, 2, 6-8, 90; proposes national convention, 9; ratification of federal constitution by, 24
Virginia plan for federal constitution, 4, 26, 33-34

Wallace, George C., 64-65
Ward, Samuel, 20
Washington, state of, petition for prayer in public schools amendment, 62
Washington Post, 63, 72
Whitten, Jamie L., 62
Wilson, James, 27, 34-35

# ABOUT THE AUTHOR

WILBUR EDEL is Professor Emeritus of Political Science, Herbert H. Lehman College, The City University of New York. He retired in 1976 from the position of Vice-President and Dean of Administration at Lehman.

Dr. Edel is author of The State Department, the Public and the United Nations. His articles on administrative and foreign policy questions have appeared in Modern Government, Educational Record, and Journal of Geography.

Dr. Edel holds a B.S. from New York University and an M.A. and Ph.D. from Columbia University.